# Better Homes and Gardens®
# FRESH FISH
## COOK BOOK

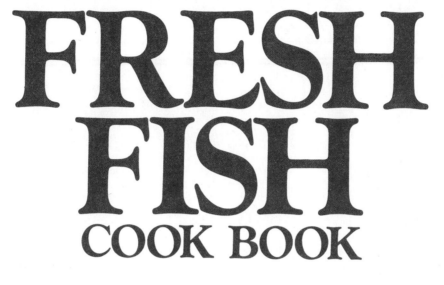

Our seal assures you that every recipe in the
*Fresh Fish Cook Book*
has been tested in the Better Homes and Gardens® Test Kitchen.
This means that each recipe is practical and
reliable, and meets our high standards of taste appeal.

**BETTER HOMES AND GARDENS® BOOKS**
Editor: Gerald M. Knox
Art Director: Ernest Shelton
Managing Editor: David A. Kirchner
Copy and Production Editors: James D. Blume, Marsha Jahns,
    Rosanne Weber Mattson, Mary Helen Schiltz

Food and Nutrition Editor: Nancy Byal
Department Head, Cook Books: Sharyl Heiken
Associate Department Heads: Sandra Granseth,
    Rosemary C. Hutchinson, Elizabeth Woolever
Senior Food Editors: Julia Malloy, Marcia Stanley, Joyce Trollope
Associate Food Editors: Linda Henry, Mary Major, Diana McMillen,
    Mary Jo Plutt, Maureen Powers, Martha Schiel,
    Linda Foley Woodrum
Recipe Development Editor: Marion Viall
Test Kitchen Director: Sharon Stilwell
Test Kitchen Photo Studio Director: Janet Pittman
Test Kitchen Home Economists: Lynn Blanchard, Jean Brekke,
    Kay Cargill, Marilyn Cornelius, Jennifer Darling,
    Maryellyn Krantz, Lynelle Munn, Dianna Nolin, Marge Steenson

Associate Art Directors: Linda Ford Vermie, Neoma Alt West,
    Randall Yontz
Assistant Art Directors: Lynda Haupert, Harijs Priekulis,
    Tom Wegner
Senior Graphic Designers: Jack Murphy, Stan Sams,
    Darla Whipple-Frain
Graphic Designers: Mike Burns, Sally Cooper, Blake Welch,
    Brian Wignall, Kimberly Zarley

Vice President, Editorial Director: Doris Eby
Executive Director, Editorial Services: Duane L. Gregg

President, Book Group: Fred Stines
Director of Publishing: Robert B. Nelson
Vice President, Retail Marketing: Jamie Martin
Vice President, Direct Marketing: Arthur Heydendael

**FRESH FISH COOK BOOK**
Editor: Mary Jo Plutt
Copy and Production Editor: James D. Blume
Graphic Designer: Blake Welch
Electronic Text Processor: Joyce Wasson
Contributing Photographers: Ron Crofoot, de Gennaro Studios,
    Mike Dieter, Scott Little
Food Stylists: Mable Hoffman, Janet Pittman, Maria Rolandelli,
    Judy Tills
Contributing Illustrator: Thomas Rosborough

**On the front cover:** Vegetable-Topped Halibut
(see recipe, page 11)

"What is it?" and "How do I cook it?" These were the two most common questions asked by customers at the local fish market where I began my research. I decided then that this book had to try to solve these fish-cooking mysteries.

To answer "What is it?" I wrote a fish selection guide, which you'll find beginning on page 88. These charts not only tell you the size, flavor, and texture of the different fishes, but also suggest substitutes—a real advantage when a particular fish is out of season.

After tackling the charts, I began developing the recipes. With the help of our Test Kitchen, I chose the cooking methods that best fit the individual characteristics of each fish. The result is a wide variety of creative dishes ranging from appetizers, to soups and stews, to main dishes. And if you're watching your diet, look for the recipes marked "Light & Low"; they're especially low in calories, sodium, fat, and cholesterol.

So before you visit the fish market again, check the *Fresh Fish Cook Book*; it will answer all of your fish-cooking questions. Then, the only question you'll have left will be, "Which recipe do I serve tonight?"

*Mary Jo Plutt*

# CATCHING THE BASICS

## Buying the Right Catch

Spotting freshness is important when shopping for fish. At the market, rely on your nose; avoid buying fish with a strong or fishy odor. Check below for other characteristics of quality.

**Fresh fish**

**1** The skin should be shiny, taut, and bright. As a fish begins to deteriorate, its colors fade.

**2** The flesh should spring back and feel firm and elastic when you lightly press it with your finger.

Fillets and steaks should have a moist, clean-cut appearance. Ragged-cut edges and discoloration indicate poor quality.

**3** The eyes should be clear, bright, and bulging. Avoid fish with dull, bloody, or sunken eyes.

**4** The gills should be red and not slippery. As a fish loses quality, its red gills fade.

**Frozen fish**

The flesh should be frozen solid. Avoid packages with torn wrappers, or those that have frost or blood visible inside or out.

## What's in A Name?

Buying the right form of fish can sometimes be confusing. Read below for some simple definitions of common terms.

A **drawn fish** is a whole fish minus its internal organs. A drawn fish may still need to be scaled (see tip, page 14).

A **dressed fish** has had its organs, scales, head, tail, and fins removed. It's ready to be cooked.

A **fish steak** is a crosscut slice from a large dressed fish. Steaks do not need any special preparation before cooking.

A **fish fillet** is a boneless piece cut lengthwise from the side and away from the backbone. If you prefer to remove the skin, see the tip on page 14.

A **frozen fish portion** is a uniform-size piece of fish cut from a large, frozen fillet block. Because of its rectangular shape and its thickness, it won't work well in many of our main-dish recipes. But thawed and cut into smaller pieces, you can use it in our soups. Or, when cooked, use it in our salads.

## How Much To Buy

How much raw fish you buy depends on its form. Buy these amounts per serving:
- 8 to 12 ounces of drawn or dressed fish
- 4 to 8 ounces of steaks or fillets
- 1 to 2 pieces of frozen fish portions

## Will It Keep?

The sooner after the catch your fresh fish is cooked, the better. But if you can't cook it right away, refrigerate or freeze it until you're ready to use it.

- **Refrigerator storage:** Wrap uncooked fish loosely in clear plastic wrap. Cook it within 2 days. Store any leftover cooked fish, covered, in the refrigerator and use it within 2 days.
- **Freezer storage:** If you're unable to cook the fish within 2 days, then freeze it. Wrap it in moisture- and vaporproof wrap. Store it at 0° or lower. Fish with a high-fat content

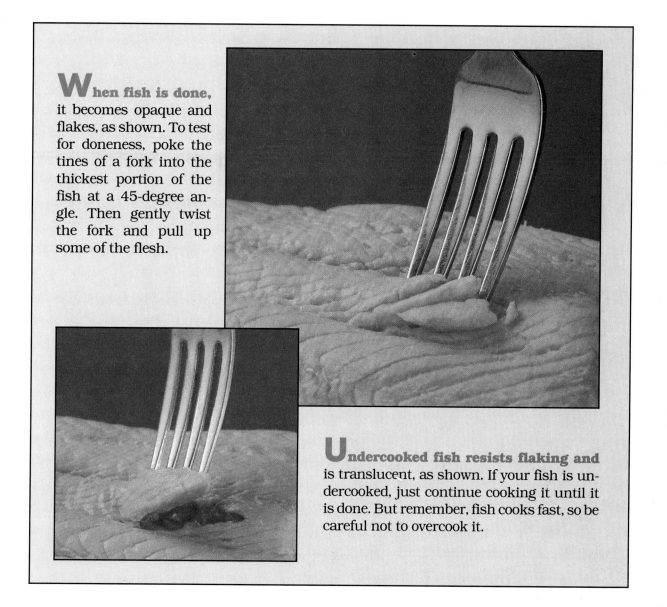

**W**hen fish is done, it becomes opaque and flakes, as shown. To test for doneness, poke the tines of a fork into the thickest portion of the fish at a 45-degree angle. Then gently twist the fork and pull up some of the flesh.

**U**ndercooked fish resists flaking and is translucent, as shown. If your fish is undercooked, just continue cooking it until it is done. But remember, fish cooks fast, so be careful not to overcook it.

will keep for up to 3 months; lean fish will keep for up to 6 months (see charts, pages 88–91).

To thaw the fish, place the unopened package of fish in the refrigerator for 6 to 8 hours. Do not thaw the fish at room temperature or in water because it will not thaw evenly and may spoil. Also, remember to *never* refreeze fish.

# Helpful Cooking Hints

### ●Minutes count
Compared with most meats, fish cooks quickly. A ½-inch-thick fillet cooks in about 5 minutes. But be careful—another minute or

two and the fish will be overcooked. Because timings are usually based on the thickness of the fish, you'll want to measure the fish at the thickest point to determine the cooking time.

### ●How done is ''done''?
Fish is properly cooked when it is opaque and flakes easily with a fork.

Undercooked fish is translucent; overcooked fish

is mealy, tough, and dry. Some fishes, such as pike and cod, flake more easily than other fishes, such as halibut and swordfish. So rely on your eye, as well as the fork, when checking doneness.

### ●Micro-cooking

The microwave recipes in this book were tested in countertop microwave ovens that operate on 600 to 700 watts. The cooking times are approximate because microwave ovens vary by manufacturer.

### ●Not all fishes are created equal

Although all fishes are a low-fat source of protein, some species have a higher fat content than others. In the charts on pages 88–91, we list each fish and whether it has a relatively low, moderate, or high fat content.

Even though all fishes can be prepared using one of the basic cooking methods on page 10, some cooking methods work better than others for particular levels of fat.

For example, low-fat fishes, with less than 5 percent fat, poach well because the liquid keeps them from drying out. When baking, broiling, micro-cooking, or grilling low-fat varieties, brush them with a sauce or with butter or margarine to keep them moist.

Moderate-fat fishes contain from 5 to 10 percent fat. These fishes adapt well to almost any method of cooking.

High-fat fishes have more than 10 percent fat. These fishes can usually be broiled, grilled, or baked without basting.

### ●Making a switch on fish

Most of our recipes give several fish options. But if these are unavailable, turn to the charts on pages 88–91. Choose a substitute fish similar in size, flavor, and texture.

First check the fat content; it's a good guide to flavor and texture. Low-fat fishes generally have a mild flavor with white or light-colored flesh. For example, you can usually substitute sole for flounder. Both are low in fat with a fine texture and a delicate flavor.

As the fat content goes up, fishes become more pronounced in flavor, firmer in texture, and darker in flesh color. For example, tuna can sometimes be used for salmon. Both are higher in fat, firmer in texture, and richer in flavor.

# Fish for Healthful Eating

Fish contains a wealth of nutrients. It's rich in protein, vitamins, and minerals, yet low in calories, fat, cholesterol, and sodium. One 3-ounce serving of a whitefish like flounder (brushed lightly with butter) contains fewer than 200 calories, 80 milligrams of cholesterol, and 210 milligrams of sodium.

For an even better nutritional bargain, choose one of our "Light & Low" recipes. They're *extra low* in calories, fat, cholesterol, and sodium. And to help guide you with your diet, check the nutrition analyses at the ends of these recipes. Listed are the U.S. Recommended Daily Allowances (U.S. RDAs) per serving.

# MAIN DISHES

Fish—it's so easy to cook!
You can poach, bake, broil,
grill, or micro-cook it.
And, no matter
which method you choose,
this chapter has the recipes
you'll need, for everything
from quick and
nutritious lunches to easy
but elegant dinners.

# Back to Cooking Basics

*Fish is fast and easy to fix, and below are seven simple ways to cook it. Use your cooked fish in one of our salad or appetizer recipes, or top it with a sauce from pages 51–54. Either way, you've got a flavorful dish in only minutes.*

**To poach fillets and steaks:** For the simmering liquid, use just enough broth, wine, water, or a combination of liquids to half-cover the fish. Bring the liquid just to boiling.

Carefully add the fish. Return just to boiling, then reduce the heat. Cover and simmer gently till done. Allow 4 to 6 minutes per ½-inch thickness of fish.

As a guide, one pound of fillets or steaks with skin will give you about 12 ounces of cooked meat.

**To poach dressed fish:** In a fish poacher pan or a large roasting pan that has a wire rack with handles, pour in enough liquid to half-cover the fish. With fish and rack *not* in the pan, bring the liquid just to boiling.

Place the fish on the greased rack of the pan. Carefully lower rack into the pan. Return just to boiling, then reduce the heat. Cover and simmer gently till done. Allow 6 to 9 minutes per ½ pound.

A 2½-pound dressed fish will give you about 1¾ pounds of cooked meat.

**To bake fillets and steaks:** Preheat the oven to 450°. Place the fish in a single layer in a greased shallow baking pan. For fillets, tuck under any thin edges. Brush fish with melted butter or margarine. Season with salt and pepper.

Bake, uncovered, in the 450° oven till done, basting with butter if necessary. Allow 4 to 6 minutes per ½-inch thickness.

**To bake dressed fish:** Preheat the oven to 350°. Place the fish in a greased baking pan. Brush the outside and the cavity of the fish with melted butter. Season. Bake, uncovered, in the 350° oven till done. Allow 6 to 9 minutes per ½ pound of fish.

**To micro-cook fillets and steaks:** Place fish in a single layer in a greased nonmetal baking dish. For fillets, tuck under any thin edges. Brush fish with melted butter, then season.

Cover with *heavy* clear plastic wrap. Vent wrap by leaving one corner of dish unsealed. Micro-cook on 100% power (high) till done.

Allow 3 to 4 minutes for ½-pound fillets (½ inch thick), 4 to 7 minutes for 1-pound fillets (½ inch thick), and 7 to 9 minutes for 1-pound steaks (¾ to 1 inch thick). For fillets, rotate the dish a half-turn after 3 minutes. For steaks, turn them over and rearrange them after 4 minutes.

**To broil fillets and steaks:** Preheat broiler. Place fish on a greased rack of an unheated broiler pan. Tuck under any thin edges. Brush with butter; season.

Broil 4 inches from the heat till done, basting with butter if necessary. Allow 4 to 6 minutes per ½-inch thickness. If fish is 1 inch or more thick, turn it over halfway through broiling.

**To grill fillets and steaks:** Place fillets in a well-greased grill basket so they won't break apart. You don't need a basket for steaks, but be sure to brush the grill rack with cooking oil so the steaks won't stick.

Grill the fish on an uncovered grill directly over *medium-hot* coals till done, seasoning and basting with butter if necessary. Allow 4 to 6 minutes per ½-inch thickness. If fish is 1 inch or more thick, turn it over halfway through grilling.

# Vegetable-Topped Halibut

*Colorful and hearty, this chunky sauce also goes well with grouper, cod, or orange roughy. (Vegetable-Topped Halibut pictured on the cover.)*

1 small yellow summer squash
1 small zucchini
1 cup sliced fresh mushrooms
½ of a small onion, sliced and separated into rings
1 clove garlic, minced
¼ teaspoon finely shredded lemon peel
6 halibut steaks, cut 1 to 1¼ inches thick (about 3 pounds)
1 14½-ounce can tomatoes
1 tablespoon cornstarch
¼ teaspoon dried basil, crushed
Dash bottled hot pepper sauce

● For sauce, cut yellow squash and zucchini lengthwise in half. Then cut into ¼-inch-thick slices. (You should have 2 cups total.) In a medium saucepan combine yellow squash, zucchini, mushrooms, onion, garlic, lemon peel, ¼ cup *water*, and ⅛ teaspoon *salt*. Bring to boiling, then reduce heat. Cover and simmer about 4 minutes or till nearly tender. Drain and return vegetables to the saucepan.

● Meanwhile, poach fish according to tip, opposite.

● To finish sauce, cut up tomatoes. Stir together *undrained* tomatoes, cornstarch, dried basil, and pepper sauce. Then add to vegetable mixture. Cook and stir gently over medium heat till thickened and bubbly. Cook and stir gently for 2 minutes more.

● To serve, spoon sauce over poached fish. If desired, garnish with fresh basil leaves. Makes 6 servings.

# Chilled Wine-Poached Steaks

*Need a cool meal on a hot summer day? Cook these steaks up to two days ahead, then top with either the Sorrel Sauce or the Avocado Sauce.*

1½ cups water
½ cup dry white wine
1 small green onion, sliced
1 bay leaf
4 cod, halibut, salmon, *or* shark steaks, cut 1 to 1¼ inches thick (about 2 pounds)
Sorrel Sauce *or* Avocado Sauce

● In a large skillet combine water, wine, green onion, and bay leaf. Bring just to boiling. Carefully add fish. Return just to boiling, then reduce heat. Cover and simmer gently for 8 to 15 minutes or till fish is done. Remove fish from water. Pat the fish dry with paper towels. Cover and chill for up to 2 days.

● To serve, spoon sauce over poached fish. Makes 4 servings.

**Sorrel Sauce:** In a small mixing bowl stir together ¼ cup plain *yogurt*, ¼ cup *mayonnaise or salad dressing*, ¼ cup finely chopped *sorrel or spinach*, 1 sliced *green onion*, ½ teaspoon prepared *horseradish*, and dash *white pepper*. If desired, cover and chill for up to 4 hours. Makes ⅔ cup.

**Avocado Sauce:** In a blender container or food processor bowl place 1 *avocado*, halved, seeded, peeled, and cut into chunks; ¼ cup *chicken broth*; 2 tablespoons *milk*; 1 tablespoon *lime juice*; 2 teaspoons grated *onion*; and dash *pepper*. Cover and blend or process just till smooth. Serve immediately. Makes ¾ cup.

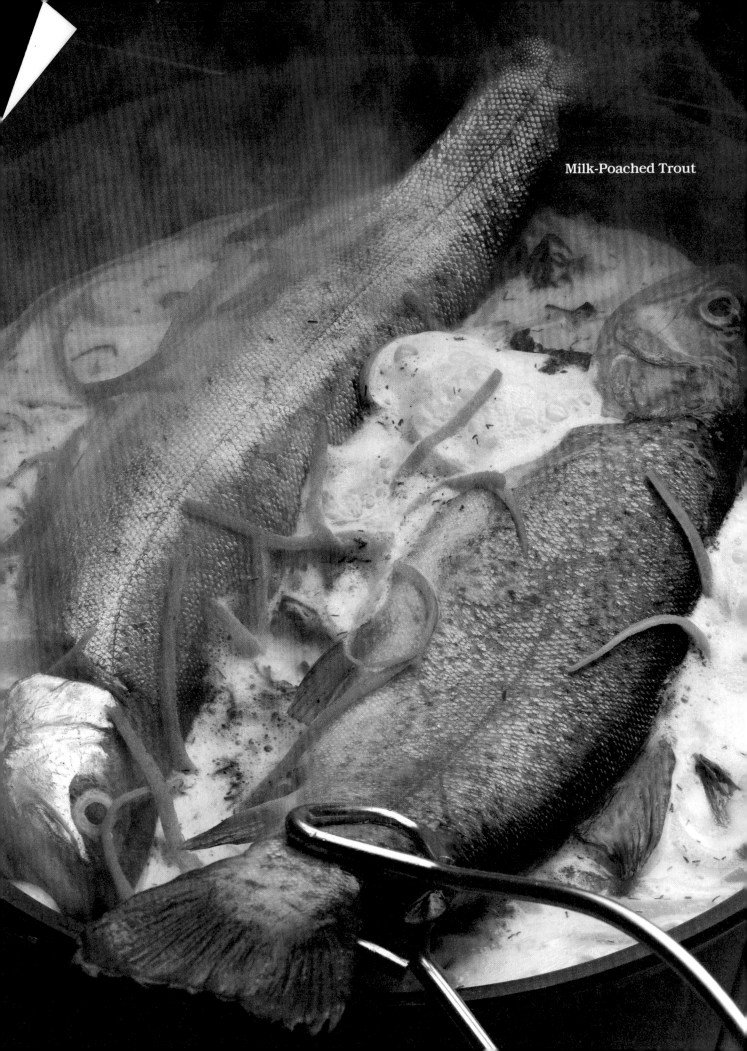

Milk-Poached Trout

# Sole Véronique

*Pronounce it vay-raw-NEEK. This classic French dish is named after the Veronica seedless grape, but any seedless grape will do.*

1 pound skinless sole,
    Atlantic ocean perch,
    cusk, flounder, *or*
    whitefish fillets
1 cup Fish Stock (see recipe,
    page 57) *or* chicken broth
⅓ cup milk
1 tablespoon all-purpose flour
½ teaspoon finely shredded
    lemon peel
    Dash ground nutmeg
½ cup seedless grapes, halved
    Watercress sprigs (optional)

● Measure thickness of fish. In a large skillet bring the Fish Stock or chicken broth just to boiling. Carefully add fish. Return just to boiling, then reduce heat. Cover and simmer gently till done (allow 4 to 6 minutes per ½-inch thickness of fish). Transfer fish to a serving platter. Cover fish to keep it warm while preparing sauce.

● For sauce, gently boil the stock or broth, uncovered, till reduced to *½ cup.* Combine milk, flour, lemon peel, and nutmeg. Then add mixture to stock or broth. Cook and stir over medium heat till thickened and bubbly, then add grapes. Cook and stir for 1 minute more. Pour sauce over fish. If desired, garnish with watercress. Makes 4 servings.

*Per serving:* 143 calories, 23 g protein, 290 mg sodium, 3 g fat, and 52 mg cholesterol.

# Milk-Poached Trout

*Use lots of vegetables and herbs to season this poaching liquid. Then add hints of sherry and paprika to enhance the flavor and color of the sauce.*

¾ cup milk
½ cup water
1 small onion, sliced and
    separated into rings
1 small carrot, cut into
    julienne sticks
¼ cup celery leaves
¾ teaspoon dried dillweed
½ teaspoon salt
⅛ teaspoon pepper
2 8- to 10-ounce scaled drawn
    rainbow trout *or* coho
    salmon
1 tablespoon cold water
1½ teaspoons cornstarch
1 tablespoon dry sherry
⅛ teaspoon paprika

● In a medium skillet combine milk, ½ cup water, onion, carrot, celery leaves, dillweed, salt, and pepper. Bring to boiling, then reduce heat. Cover and simmer for 10 minutes.

● Carefully add fish. Return just to boiling; reduce heat. Cover and simmer gently for 6 to 10 minutes or till done. Remove fish from skillet. Cover fish to keep it warm while preparing sauce.

● For sauce, line a colander with cheesecloth. Pour cooking liquid through colander. Discard solids. Place *½ cup* of the strained liquid in a saucepan (add water if necessary). Combine 1 tablespoon water and cornstarch. Then add it to the strained liquid. Cook and stir till thickened and bubbly. Cook and stir for 2 minutes more. Remove from heat. Stir in sherry and paprika.

● To serve, pull the fins from each fish. Arrange fish on dinner plates. Spoon some sauce onto the plates, next to fish. Pass the remaining sauce. Makes 2 servings.

# Perfect Preparation

*Making a trip to the fish market may not be as much fun as going fishing, but it's a lot quicker. And since most markets will do the cleaning for you, it's easier, too. But you'll still need to know a few simple before-cooking tips.*

To remove the scales from a whole or drawn fish (see "What's in a Name?", page 6), first wet the fish, then firmly grasp the tail with one hand. With the other hand, use a scaler or a dull knife to scrape from tail to head. Use short, swift strokes until you've removed all of the scales.

Rinse drawn fish under cold running water. Then check the abdominal cavity to make sure that all of the guts have been removed. If necessary, cut away any remaining guts with a small sharp knife and rinse the fish again.

To remove the skin from a fillet, place the fillet with the skin side down on a cutting board. Starting at the tail end, insert a sharp knife between the meat and the skin. Firmly holding the skin on the cutting surface, use a sawing motion to cut the meat from the skin.

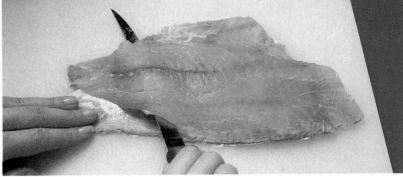

*Whether you're enjoying a single-serving-size fish or presenting one to feed a crowd, follow these four easy steps to remove the skin and bones from your cooked drawn fish:*
Using the tip of a sharp knife, cut through the flesh along the center of the backbone from head to tail.

To remove the skin from the fish, make cuts at the base of the head and at the base of the tail, cutting at right angles to the backbone. Using the knife and a fork, loosen and gently pull the skin toward the stomach to peel it off.

For a single-serving fish, use the fork to lift the top fillet away from the backbone.

For a larger fish, cut the fillet into serving portions before removing it from the backbone. Then place the portions on the platter.

Pull away the thick backbone and discard it. This will expose the bottom layer of the fish. Use the fork or a server to remove the bottom fillet from the skin underneath.

# Japanese-Style Steamed Fish

*The ginger-soy sauce adds kick to this lemony fish.*

2  8- to 12-ounce scaled drawn
porgies, flounder, *or*
rainbow trout, *or* four
4-ounce butterfish
4  lemon slices
2  tablespoons snipped chives
1½  cups small whole fresh
mushrooms
2  tablespoons soy sauce
1  tablespoon lemon juice
1  tablespoon water
1  teaspoon grated gingerroot

● In a large skillet place a large open steamer basket over 1 inch *water*. Bring water to boiling, then reduce heat to a simmer. Carefully place fish on the steamer basket. Top with lemon slices and chives, then add mushrooms.

● Cover skillet. Steam for 8 to 15 minutes or till fish is done.

● Meanwhile, for the dipping sauce, combine soy sauce, lemon juice, water, and gingerroot. Serve the sauce on the side with the steamed fish and mushrooms. Makes 2 servings.

# Trout with Tarragon-Cream Sauce

*If your wire rack doesn't have handles, put two or three strips of heavy or triple-thickness foil underneath the fish.*

Water
2  lemon slices
1  2- to 2½-pound dressed lake
trout, sea trout, *or* pike
Salt
Tarragon-Cream Sauce

● In a fish poacher pan or a large roasting pan that has a wire rack with handles, pour in enough water to almost reach the rack. Then add lemon slices. With the fish and rack *not* in the pan, bring water to boiling. Then reduce heat to a simmer.

● Sprinkle the fish with salt and place it on the greased rack. Carefully lower the rack into the pan. Cover pan. Steam for 20 to 25 minutes or till fish is done.

● Meanwhile, prepare Tarragon-Cream Sauce. Lift rack with fish from pan. Use 2 wide spatulas to carefully transfer the fish to a serving platter. Pass sauce with fish. Makes 5 or 6 servings.

**Tarragon-Cream Sauce:** In a small saucepan combine ⅓ cup *dry white wine* and 3 tablespoons finely chopped *shallots or* thinly sliced *green onion*. Bring to boiling, then reduce heat. Simmer, uncovered, for 8 to 10 minutes or till liquid is reduced to about *3 tablespoons*, stirring occasionally.
● Combine 1 cup *light cream* and 4 teaspoons *all-purpose flour*. Then stir it into wine mixture along with ⅛ teaspoon *salt*; ⅛ teaspoon dried *tarragon*, crushed; ⅛ teaspoon *pepper*. Cook and stir over medium heat till thickened and bubbly. Cook and stir for 1 minute more. Makes 1¼ cups.

# Pike and Shrimp Quenelles

*The small oval quenelles (pronounced kuh-NELLS) look a little like dumplings, but they're more delicate. Serve them as a first course or as a light main dish.*

4 ounces fresh *or* frozen
    shelled shrimp
4 ounces skinless pike *or*
    flounder fillets
1 cup cold whipping cream
2 egg whites
¼ teaspoon dried dillweed
⅛ teaspoon salt
    Dash pepper
2 cups hot Fish Stock (see
    recipe, page 57) *or* hot
    water *plus* ½ teaspoon
    salt
    Mushroom Sauce
    Paprika
    Parsley sprigs

● Thaw shrimp, if frozen. Devein shrimp. Pat dry with paper towels. Coarsely chop shrimp and fish. In a blender container or food processor bowl place *half* of the shrimp, *half* of the fish, and *1 tablespoon* of the cream. Cover and blend or process till smooth, stopping to scrape sides as needed. Remove the mixture and set aside. Repeat with remaining shrimp and fish and with *1 tablespoon* cream. Return all to container or bowl.

● Add egg whites, dillweed, ⅛ teaspoon salt, and pepper. Cover and blend or process for 5 seconds or till mixture thickens into a paste. Through the opening in the lid or with lid ajar, and with blender on slow speed, *gradually* add remaining cream. Blend or process for 30 to 60 seconds more or till thick, stopping to scrape sides as needed. Cover and chill for 2 hours.

● Grease a 12-inch skillet. To shape quenelles, dip 2 metal soup spoons into a small bowl of hot water. Using 1 of the hot wet spoons, scoop out about *2 tablespoons* of the fish mixture. Use the second hot wet spoon to form the mixture into a smooth, oval mound. Carefully transfer quenelle to the skillet. Repeat with remaining mixture, making a total of 16. Dip spoons in hot water before the shaping of each quenelle.

● Gently pour hot Fish Stock or salted hot water down the side of the skillet. Bring just to boiling, then reduce heat. Cover and simmer gently about 10 minutes or till set and light textured.

● Meanwhile, prepare Mushroom Sauce. Cover sauce to keep it warm. Using a slotted spoon, remove the quenelles from skillet. Drain on paper towels.

● To serve, transfer quenelles to individual plates. Spoon sauce over quenelles and sprinkle with paprika. Garnish with parsley sprigs. Makes 4 main-dish or 8 appetizer servings.

**Mushroom Sauce:** In a saucepan melt 1 tablespoon *butter or margarine*. Add ¼ cup finely chopped fresh *mushrooms*. Cook for 3 to 4 minutes or till tender. Stir in 1 tablespoon *all-purpose flour* and ⅛ teaspoon *salt*. Add ¾ cup *milk*. Cook and stir over medium heat till thickened and bubbly. Stir in 1 tablespoon *dry sherry*. Cook and stir for 1 minute more. Makes ¾ cup.

# Mustard-Topped Pompano en Papillote

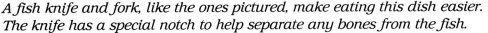

*A fish knife and fork, like the ones pictured, make eating this dish easier.*
*The knife has a special notch to help separate any bones from the fish.*

1 medium carrot, cut into
   julienne sticks
½ pound skinless pompano,
   flounder, *or* orange
   roughy fillets
2 15x12-inch pieces
   parchment paper
2 teaspoons Dijon-style
   mustard
¼ teaspoon dried basil,
   crushed
1 small zucchini, sliced
   ¼ inch thick (1 cup)
   Dash garlic powder
   Dash salt
   Pepper
   Snipped chives

● In a covered saucepan cook the carrot in a small amount of boiling water about 4 minutes or till nearly tender, then drain.

● Meanwhile, measure thickness of fish; cut it into 2 portions.

● To assemble fish bundles, see the tip on page 20. Cut heart shapes from parchment, then open. For each bundle, place a fish portion on the right half of a heart, tucking under any thin edges of the fish. (If fish is less than ½ inch thick, stack fillets to about ½ inch thickness.) Spread mustard over fish. Sprinkle with basil. Top with the carrot and zucchini. Sprinkle with garlic powder, salt, and pepper, then with chives.

● Fold left half of each heart over fish. Starting at the top, seal each bundle by folding edges together. Twist tip of heart to hold bundle closed. Place bundles on an ungreased baking sheet. Bake in a 450° oven for 12 to 15 minutes or till paper puffs up and fish is done *(carefully* open paper to check doneness).

● To serve, cut bundles open by slashing a large X on the top of each, then pull back the paper. Transfer bundles to dinner plates. Makes 2 servings.

**To micro-cook:** Prepare Mustard-Topped Pompano en Papillote as directed above, *except* place carrot in a small microwave-safe bowl. Add 2 tablespoons *water.* Cover with vented clear plastic wrap. Micro-cook carrot on 100% power (high) about 2 minutes or till nearly tender.
● Assemble fish bundles. Place bundles on a large microwave-safe plate. Cook on high for 2 minutes. Rotate bundles a half-turn and cook on high for 2 to 4 minutes more or till paper puffs up and fish is done.

*Per serving:* 123 calories, 20 g protein, 319 mg sodium, 1 g fat, and 57 mg cholesterol.

Mustard-Topped
Pompano en Papillote

# Honey-Curried Trout Bundles

*Would you rather cook the bundles in your microwave? Use the directions for Mustard-Topped Pompano en Papillote on page 18.*

4 ounces broccoli
1 tablespoon Dijon-style
  mustard
2 teaspoons honey
¼ teaspoon finely shredded
  lemon peel
⅛ teaspoon curry powder
2 15x12-inch pieces
  parchment paper
2 4-ounce skinless sea trout,
  orange roughy, red
  snapper, *or* salmon fillets
  (about ½ inch thick)
2 tablespoons chopped
  peanuts

● Remove outer leaves and tough parts from broccoli. Cut the broccoli stalks crosswise into ¼-inch-thick slices, then break flowerets into smaller pieces. (You should have about 1 cup total.) In a covered saucepan cook broccoli in a small amount of boiling water for 4 to 5 minutes or till nearly tender, then drain.

● Combine mustard, honey, lemon peel, and curry powder. To assemble the bundles, see the tip below. Cut heart shapes from parchment, then open. For each bundle, place a fillet on right side of a heart, tucking under any thin edges of the fish. Spread with mustard mixture; top with broccoli and nuts.

● Fold left half of each heart over fish. Starting at the top, seal each bundle by folding edges together. Twist tip of heart to hold bundle closed. Place bundles on an ungreased baking sheet. Bake in a 450° oven about 10 minutes or till paper puffs up and fish is done *(carefully* open paper to check doneness). Serves 2.

*Per serving:* 221 calories, 24 g protein, 286 mg sodium, 9 g fat, and 57 mg cholesterol.

## Cooking in Paper

"En papillote" (poppy-YOTE) is a simple yet elegant method of cooking. To assemble each package:
**1.** Fold the parchment paper in half. Then cut a half-heart shape 6 inches longer and 2 inches wider than the fish. (The fold will be the center of the heart.)
**2.** Open each paper heart and arrange one piece of fish and toppings on the right half of the heart.
**3.** Fold the left half of the heart over the fish, matching edges. Starting at the top of the heart, seal the package by folding the edges together in a double fold. Fold only a small section at a time to ensure a tight seal. Then twist the tip of the heart to close the package.

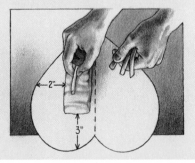

# Cordon Bleu Stacked Fillets

*A takeoff on chicken cordon bleu, featuring ham and Swiss cheese between fish fillets.*

8 3- to 3½-ounce skinless flounder *or* sole fillets
4 slices boiled ham
2 slices Swiss cheese, quartered
1 green onion, thinly sliced
1 egg
1 tablespoon water
¼ cup fine dry seasoned bread crumbs
1 tablespoon grated Parmesan cheese
1 tablespoon snipped parsley

● Place *half* of the fillets on a greased wire rack in a shallow baking pan. Top each fillet with a piece of ham, cutting ham to fit fillet. Place 2 pieces of cheese on ham, then sprinkle with green onion.

● In a shallow dish combine egg and water. In another shallow dish combine bread crumbs, Parmesan cheese, and parsley. Dip *1 side* of the remaining fillets into egg mixture, then dip into the crumb mixture. With the crumb side up, form sandwiches by placing the crumb-coated fillets on top of the other fillets in the pan. Sprinkle with any remaining crumb mixture.

● Bake in a 450° oven about 10 minutes or till fish is done. Makes 4 servings.

**To micro-cook:** Prepare the Cordon Bleu Stacked Fillets as directed above, *except* place fillets on a nonmetal rack in a 12x7½x2-inch baking dish. Micro-cook, uncovered, on 100% power (high) for 4 minutes. Rotate dish a half-turn and cook, uncovered, on high for 2 to 4 minutes more or till fish is done.

# Corn Breaded Fish Bake

*Fish olé! Mexican corn bread and salsa give this dish a south-of-the-border flavor.*

1 pound skinless cod, pollack, *or* whitefish fillets
1½ cups yellow cornmeal
¾ teaspoon baking soda
¾ teaspoon salt
1¼ cups shredded cheddar cheese (5 ounces)
1 4-ounce can diced green chili peppers, drained
2 eggs
1 cup buttermilk
¼ cup shortening, melted, *or* cooking oil
Dash bottled hot pepper sauce
Paprika
Green Chili Salsa, heated (see recipe, page 53)

● If necessary, cut fillets to about ½-inch thickness. Then cut into about 4x1-inch strips. Cover and refrigerate till needed.

● In a large mixing bowl stir together the cornmeal, soda, and salt. Stir in *1 cup* of the cheese and the chili peppers. In another mixing bowl combine eggs, buttermilk, melted shortening or cooking oil, and hot pepper sauce. Beat egg mixture with a rotary beater till well combined, then add it to the cornmeal mixture. Stir till mixture is smooth.

● Spread *half* of the batter in a greased 9x9x2-inch baking pan. Place fish in rows on top of batter. Then spread remaining batter over fish and sprinkle with paprika.

● Bake in a 450° oven about 20 minutes or till a toothpick inserted in corn bread center comes out clean. Sprinkle with remaining cheese; bake for 1 to 2 minutes more or till melted.

● To serve, cut into squares and top with warm Green Chili Salsa. Makes 6 servings.

Pizza-Baked Rockfish

# Pizza-Baked Rockfish

½ cup sliced fresh mushrooms
¼ cup chopped onion
¼ cup water
3 tablespoons sodium-free tomato paste
½ teaspoon dried basil, crushed
½ teaspoon dried oregano, crushed
¼ teaspoon sugar
¼ teaspoon fennel seed
⅛ teaspoon crushed red pepper
1 clove garlic, minced
 Nonstick spray coating
8 ounces skinless rockfish *or* red snapper fillets
4 green pepper rings
½ cup shredded mozzarella cheese (2 ounces)

● For sauce, in a small saucepan combine *half* of the mushrooms, onion, water, tomato paste, basil, oregano, sugar, fennel seed, red pepper, and garlic. Bring to boiling, then reduce heat. Simmer, uncovered, for 4 minutes, stirring the mixture occasionally. Remove from heat.

● Meanwhile, spray 2 shallow individual casseroles with the nonstick coating. Measure thickness of fish. Cut it into 2 equal portions. Place fish in casseroles, tucking under any thin edges.

● Spoon the sauce over fish. Top with remaining mushrooms, green pepper, and cheese. Bake in a 450° oven till fish is done (allow 5 to 7 minutes per ½-inch thickness). Makes 2 servings.

*Per serving:* 222 calories, 30 g protein, 224 mg sodium, 7 g fat, and 55 mg cholesterol.

# Snowcapped Grouper

*Serve steamed broccoli on the side as a colorful companion to this puffy egg-topped fish.*

 Nonstick spray coating
1 pound skinless grouper, salmon, sea bass, *or* tilefish fillets (½ to ¾ inch thick)
1 tablespoon all-purpose flour
2 egg whites
¼ cup reduced-calorie mayonnaise *or* salad dressing
½ teaspoon dry mustard
3 tablespoons grated Parmesan cheese

● Spray a 12x7½x2-inch baking dish with nonstick coating. Cut fish into 4 equal portions. Dip fish into flour, then place portions in the baking dish, tucking under any thin edges.

● For egg topping, beat egg whites till stiff peaks form (tips stand straight.) Combine mayonnaise or salad dressing and mustard, then fold it into egg whites. Spoon egg topping on fish. Sprinkle with cheese. Bake in a 350° oven for 25 to 30 minutes or till topping is golden and fish is done. Makes 4 servings.

**To micro-cook:** Prepare Snowcapped Grouper as above, *except* do not dip fish in flour. Place fish in dish. Cover with vented plastic wrap. Micro-cook on 100% power (high) for 3 minutes. Rotate dish a half-turn. Cook on high for 2 to 4 minutes or till done; drain. Spoon on egg topping. Sprinkle with cheese. Cook, uncovered, on 50% power (medium) for 8 to 10 minutes or till egg is soft-set, rotating dish a quarter-turn every 3 minutes.

*Per serving:* 184 calories, 26 g protein, 287 mg sodium, 7 g fat, and 59 mg cholesterol.

# Cheesy Pick-Your-Fish Potpies

*In a hurry? Then use purchased plain croutons as the top "crust" for these individual pies.*

1½ pounds skinless firm-
   textured fillets (see
   charts, pages 88–91)
¼ cup butter *or* margarine
⅓ cup all-purpose flour
1 teaspoon instant chicken
   bouillon granules
1½ cups milk
1 cup shredded American
   cheese (4 ounces)
2 tablespoons diced pimiento
¼ teaspoon bottled hot pepper
   sauce
2 cups loose-pack frozen
   mixed broccoli, carrots,
   and cauliflower, thawed
1 8-ounce can whole water
   chestnuts, drained and
   cut up
1 cup Dill Croutons (see
   tip, page 70)

● Cut fish into ½-inch pieces. Cover and refrigerate till needed.

● For cheese mixture, in a medium saucepan melt butter or margarine. Stir in flour and bouillon granules. Add milk. Cook and stir over medium heat till thickened and bubbly. Add the cheese, pimiento, and hot pepper sauce. Stir till cheese melts, then remove from heat.

● Add fish, mixed vegetables, and water chestnuts. Stir lightly to coat. Transfer mixture to six 10-ounce casseroles. Bake in a 400° oven for 10 to 15 minutes or till fish is done. Sprinkle croutons on top and serve. Makes 6 servings.

# Red Snapper Veracruz

1 medium onion, chopped
3 cloves garlic, minced
¼ cup water
1 16-ounce can tomatoes,
   cut up
⅓ cup sliced pitted green *or*
   ripe olives
1 tablespoon lime juice
1 to 2 teaspoons chopped
   canned jalapeño chili
   peppers
1 teaspoon sugar
1 pound skinless red snapper
   fillets (about ½ inch thick)
   Hot cooked rice

● For sauce, in a saucepan combine onion, garlic, and water. Bring to boiling; reduce heat. Cover and cook about 2 minutes or till tender. Stir in *undrained* tomatoes, olives, lime juice, peppers, and sugar. Return to boiling; reduce heat. Simmer, covered, for 5 minutes. Uncover and simmer for 10 minutes.

● Meanwhile, place fillets in a 12x7½x2-inch baking dish, tucking under any thin edges. Spoon sauce on top. Bake in a 450° oven for 8 to 10 minutes or till fish is done. Transfer fish and sauce to a serving platter. Serve with rice. Makes 4 servings.

**To micro-cook:** Prepare Red Snapper Veracruz as directed above, *except* omit water. Stir the sauce ingredients together in a 4-cup glass measure. Cover with vented clear plastic wrap. Then micro-cook on 100% power (high) for 8 to 10 minutes or till onion is tender, stirring every 2 minutes. Set aside.
● To cook fish, cover baking dish with vented clear plastic wrap. Cook on high for 3 minutes. Rotate dish a half-turn and cook on high, covered, for 1 to 4 minutes more or till fish is done. Transfer fish to a platter, then spoon sauce over fish. Serve with rice.

# Ratatouille-Topped Fillets

1½ cups cubed peeled eggplant
2 medium tomatoes, seeded and chopped
1 8-ounce can reduced-sodium tomato sauce
1 small onion, thinly sliced and separated into rings
½ of a small zucchini, sliced ¼ inch thick (½ cup)
½ cup sliced fresh mushrooms
½ cup chopped green pepper
½ teaspoon dried basil, crushed
¼ teaspoon garlic powder
¼ teaspoon dried oregano, crushed
⅛ teaspoon salt
Nonstick spray coating
1 pound skinless flounder, haddock, orange roughy, or sole fillets

● For vegetable mixture, in a medium saucepan combine the eggplant, chopped tomatoes, tomato sauce, onion, zucchini, mushrooms, green pepper, basil, garlic powder, oregano, and salt. Bring the mixture to boiling, then reduce heat. Cover and simmer for 15 minutes. Uncover and simmer about 12 minutes more or till mixture is thickened.

● Meanwhile, spray a 12x7½x2-inch baking dish with non-stick coating. Measure thickness of fish. Sprinkle with *pepper*. If using large fillets, place them in a single layer in the baking dish, tucking under any thin edges. If using small fillets, stack them evenly in the baking dish.

● Spoon vegetable mixture over fish. Cover with foil. Bake in a 450° oven till fish is done (allow 6 to 8 minutes per ½-inch thickness). Transfer to a serving platter. Makes 4 servings.

*Per serving:* 141 calories, 19 g protein, 224 mg sodium, 1 g fat, and 55 mg cholesterol.

## Evenly cooking fillets

Fillets cook more evenly if you turn under any thin edges. This makes the fillets about the same thickness so that the thinner ends won't get done before the thicker ends.

If you're using small, thin fillets such as sole or flounder in the Ratatouille-Topped Fillets, you'll need to stack them so they'll all fit in the dish. But keep in mind that, for even cooking of the fish, the fillets should be stacked to about the same thickness.

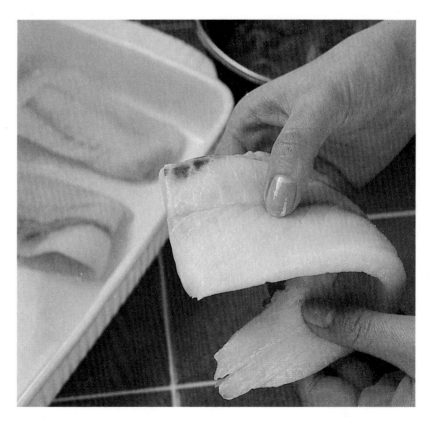

# Bacon-Stuffed Flounder Rolls

3 slices bacon
  Butter *or* margarine, melted
1 6-ounce package San Fran-
    cisco-style stuffing mix
¼ cup finely chopped onion
2 tablespoons snipped parsley
6 4-ounce skinless flounder,
    sole, *or* walleyed pike
    fillets
  Leaf lettuce
  Seedless red grapes
  Cheddar Cheese Sauce

● For stuffing, cook the bacon till crisp. Drain, reserving the drippings. Crumble bacon; set aside. Measure drippings, then add enough melted butter or margarine to equal ¼ *cup.* Prepare stuffing mix according to package directions, *except* use the dripping mixture instead of plain butter and add the onion with the water. Stir in bacon and parsley. Cool about 15 minutes.

● For rolls, cut fillets lengthwise in half. Lay 2 pieces end to end, overlapping the thinner ends. Repeat with remaining fillets. Place ⅓ *cup* stuffing onto one end of each pair of pieces. Roll fish around stuffing. Secure with wooden toothpicks. Place rolls upright in a 12x7½x2-inch baking dish. Brush with additional butter. Bake in a 375° oven about 20 minutes or till done.

● To serve, transfer rolls to a platter. Remove toothpicks. Garnish with lettuce and grapes. Then spoon on sauce. Serves 6.

**Cheddar Cheese Sauce:** In a saucepan melt 2 tablespoons *butter or margarine.* Stir in 2 tablespoons *all-purpose flour* and ¼ teaspoon *salt.* Add 1¼ cups *milk.* Cook and stir till thickened and bubbly. Cook and stir for 1 minute more. Add 1 cup shredded *cheddar cheese;* stir till melted. Makes 1½ cups.

# Apricot and Rice Rolls

¾ cup water
¼ cup long grain rice
2 tablespoons snipped dried
    apricots
1½ teaspoons instant chicken
    bouillon granules
  Dash pepper
4 3-ounce skinless flounder,
    sole, *or* walleyed pike
    fillets
  Nonstick spray coating
2 tablespoons frozen orange
    juice concentrate, thawed
2 tablespoons butter *or*
    margarine, melted
  Dash ground ginger

● For stuffing, in a saucepan combine water, *uncooked* rice, apricots, bouillon granules, and pepper. Bring to boiling; reduce heat. Cover with a tight-fitting lid. Cook for 15 minutes. Remove from heat. Let stand, covered, for 10 minutes. For rolls, spread stuffing evenly on top of fillets. Roll up each fillet jelly-roll style, starting from narrow end. Secure with wooden toothpicks.

● Spray a 12x7½x2-inch baking dish with nonstick coating. Place rolls, seam side down, in dish. Combine juice concentrate, butter or margarine, and ginger. Brush *half* over the rolls. Bake in a 375° oven for 20 to 25 minutes or till done. Remove the toothpicks. Brush with remaining butter mixture. Serves 4.

**To micro-cook:** Prepare Apricot and Rice Rolls as above, *except* cover dish with vented clear plastic wrap. Micro-cook on 100% power (high) for 3 minutes. Rotate dish a half-turn and cook, covered, on high for 3 to 5 minutes more or till done.

*Per serving:* 209 calories, 22 g protein, 290 mg sodium, 8 g fat, and 64 mg cholesterol.

Bacon-Stuffed Flounder Rolls

# Spinach-Filled Pinwheels with Mustard Sauce

*A new twist to fish rolls: Slice them to show off the green and white pinwheel pattern.*

1  10-ounce package frozen chopped spinach
¼  cup thinly sliced green onion
1  beaten egg
⅓  cup fine dry bread crumbs
1  pound skinless flounder, salmon, sole, *or* whitefish fillets (¼ to ½ inch thick)
2  tablespoons butter *or* margarine, melted
   Mustard Sauce

● For filling, cook spinach with the onion according to package directions, then drain well. In a medium mixing bowl combine cooked spinach-onion mixture and egg. Stir in bread crumbs.

● Measure length of fillets. Cut long fillets or overlap thinner ends of 2 short fillets to about 7 inches in length. For pinwheels, spread filling on top of fillets. Roll fish up jelly-roll style, starting from narrow ends. Skewer with wooden toothpicks at 1-inch intervals. Then cut the rolls between toothpicks into 1-inch-thick slices. Place the pinwheels upright in a 12x7½x2-inch baking dish. Brush with butter or margarine. Cover with foil. Bake in a 450° oven for 10 to 15 minutes or till fish is done.

● To serve, carefully remove the toothpicks from the fish. Serve with Mustard Sauce. Makes 4 servings.

**Mustard Sauce:** Whip ⅓ cup *whipping cream* till soft peaks form. Combine 2 tablespoons *mayonnaise or salad dressing* and 1 tablespoon *Dijon-style mustard,* then fold it into the whipped cream. Cover and chill for up to 1 hour. Makes ½ cup.

# Salmon-Filled Fillets

*A tip from our Test Kitchen: Use smaller fillets for a more elegant presentation.*

4  ounces skinless salmon fillet, cut into 1-inch pieces
¼  teaspoon salt
   Dash white pepper
1  egg white
½  cup cold whipping cream
1  tablespoon snipped chives
8  2½- to 3-ounce skinless flounder, sole, *or* walleyed pike fillets
1  tablespoon butter *or* margarine, melted
   Citrus-Almond Sauce (see recipe, page 51)

● For filling, in a blender container or food processor bowl place salmon, salt, and pepper. Cover and blend or process to a fine paste. Add egg white. Cover and blend or process for 5 seconds. Through the opening in the lid or with lid ajar, and with blender on slow speed, *gradually* add cream. Blend or process for 30 to 60 seconds more or till thick, stopping to scrape the sides as needed. Stir in the snipped chives and set aside.

● To fill fillets, place 4 fillets in a greased 12x7½x2-inch baking dish. Spread filling evenly on top of these fillets. Form sandwiches by placing remaining fillets on top. Brush with melted butter or margarine. Bake in a 350° oven for 15 to 20 minutes or till done. Serve with Citrus-Almond Sauce. Serves 4.

**To micro-cook:** Prepare the Salmon-Filled Fillets as directed above, *except* cover dish loosely with waxed paper. Micro-cook on 100% power (high) for 4 minutes. Carefully rearrange filled fillets, moving the outside ones to the center of the dish. Cook, loosely covered, on high for 3 to 4 minutes more or till done.

# Mexican Oven-Fried Fish

*Our Green Chili Salsa will taste peppier if it's heated first. Or you can opt for a purchased salsa and choose the mild or hot kind.*

1 pound skinless firm-textured lean fillets (½ to ¾ inch thick) (see charts, pages 88–91)
1 tablespoon butter *or* margarine
1 teaspoon chili powder
¼ cup finely crushed plain tortilla chips
  Cilantro sprigs *or* peeled avocado slices (optional)
  Green Chili Salsa (see recipe, page 53)

● Place the fillets in a well-greased shallow baking dish, tucking under any thin edges.

● In a small saucepan melt butter or margarine. Stir in chili powder. Cook and stir over medium heat for 1 minute. Brush butter mixture on top of fish. Top with crushed chips, pressing lightly so they'll stick. Bake in a 450° oven for 6 to 12 minutes or till fish is done.

● To serve, transfer to a serving platter. If desired, garnish with cilantro or avocado. Serve with Green Chili Salsa. Serves 4.

# Lemony Almond-Topped Fillets

*No time to cook? Use the microwave version for a delicious dinner in only minutes.*

1 pound skinless flounder, lake trout, orange roughy, *or* sole fillets
½ cup fine dry bread crumbs
2 tablespoons butter *or* margarine, melted
1 teaspoon finely shredded lemon peel
⅓ cup sliced almonds
  Lemon wedges (optional)

● Measure thickness of fish. If using large fillets, place them in a single layer in a lightly greased 10x6x2-inch baking dish, tucking under any of the thin edges. If using small fillets, stack them evenly in the baking dish.

● For crumb mixture, in a small mixing bowl combine bread crumbs, butter or margarine, and lemon peel. Stir till well mixed. Sprinkle the crumb mixture on top of fish, then top with almonds. Bake in a 450° oven till fish is done and crumbs are golden (allow 6 to 8 minutes per ½-inch thickness of fish). If desired, serve with lemon wedges. Makes 4 servings.

**To micro-cook:** Toast the almonds, if desired. Prepare Lemony Almond-Topped Fillets as directed above, *except* cover with vented clear plastic wrap. Then micro-cook on 100% power (high) for 3 minutes. Rotate dish a half-turn and cook, covered, on high for 2 to 4 minutes more or till fish is done.

# Easy Halibut Wellington

1 cup finely chopped fresh mushrooms
1 green onion, sliced
1 tablespoon butter *or* margarine
1 beaten egg yolk
¼ teaspoon dried dillweed
Dash salt
Dash pepper
4 halibut, shark, *or* swordfish steaks, cut 1 inch thick (1¼ pounds)
1 package (8) refrigerated crescent rolls
1 slightly beaten egg white

● For filling, in a small saucepan cook mushrooms and green onion in butter or margarine for 4 to 5 minutes or till vegetables are tender, stirring constantly. Remove from heat and cool slightly. Stir in egg yolk, dillweed, salt, and pepper. Set aside.

● Remove skin and bones from fish. In a medium skillet bring ½ cup *water* just to boiling. Carefully add fish. Return just to boiling, then reduce the heat. Cover and simmer gently for 6 minutes (fish will *not* be done). Remove fish from water. Pat fish dry with paper towels.

● Unroll crescent rolls. Seal perforations to form 4 rectangles. On a lightly floured surface roll each into a rectangle about 2 inches longer and 2 inches wider than the steaks.

● To assemble, place fish in a greased shallow baking pan. Spoon the mushroom filling on top. Then top with the pastry rectangles, tucking the pastry edges under about ½ inch. (To prevent sogginess, do not wrap entire steak in pastry.) Brush with egg white. Bake in a 425° oven about 10 minutes or till pastry is golden brown and fish is done. Makes 4 servings.

# Salmon en Croûte

1 10-ounce package frozen chopped spinach
2 green onions, sliced
1 tablespoon butter *or* margarine
¼ cup fine dry seasoned bread crumbs
1 beaten egg yolk
2 ¾-pound skinless salmon fillets (¾ to 1 inch thick)
½ of a 17½-ounce package (1 sheet) frozen puff pastry, thawed
1 beaten egg
1 tablespoon water
Cucumber-Dill Sauce *or* Blender Hollandaise Sauce (see recipes, pages 53 and 54)

● For filling, cook spinach according to package directions. Drain well, pressing out excess liquid. In a skillet cook the green onions in butter or margarine till tender but not brown. Stir in bread crumbs and egg yolk, then stir in spinach.

● In a large skillet bring 2 cups *water* just to boiling. Carefully add fish. Return just to boiling, then reduce heat. Cover and simmer gently for 2 minutes (fish will *not* be done). Remove fish from water. Pat fish dry with paper towels.

● On a floured surface roll pastry into a rectangle about 4 inches longer than length of a fillet. Lay fillets side by side; measure width. Roll pastry to twice the width *plus* 2 inches.

● To assemble, transfer pastry to an ungreased 15x10x1-inch baking pan. On *half* of the rectangle, spread *half* of the filling to within 1 inch of edges. Top with fish, then with remaining filling. Combine egg and water, then brush some onto pastry edges. Bring pastry over fish. Seal edges with the tines of a fork. Brush top with remaining egg mixture. Bake in a 400° oven for 20 to 25 minutes or till golden. Serve with sauce. Serves 6.

*Impress dinner guests with Salmon en Croûte—salmon and spinach enclosed in a flaky crust.*

## 1 Assembling the salmon bundle

Transfer the rolled-out pastry to an ungreased 15x10x1-inch baking pan, laying it across an edge as shown at right. Spread *half* of the filling over *half* of the rectangle to within 1 inch of the edges. Place the fillets on top of the filling, fitting the fillets together to form a rectangle. Then spread the remaining filling evenly over both fillets.

## 2 Sealing the pastry

Brush the egg-water mixture onto the edges of the pastry. (The mixture helps keep the pastry firmly sealed.) Then bring the pastry over to cover the fish. If necessary, trim the edges so they meet evenly. Seal by pressing edges together with the tines of a fork.

# Butterfish with Apples

*Butterfish: as delicate as butter, but with a mild, nutlike flavor.*

2 medium apples, cored and
    cut into thin wedges
3 tablespoons butter *or*
    margarine
8 6- to 8-ounce scaled drawn
    butterfish, *or* four 8- to
    12-ounce scaled drawn
    porgies *or* rainbow trout
    Apple juice *or* apple cider
    (about 2 cups)
1 green onion, thinly sliced
1 tablespoon all-purpose flour
½ cup milk
1 tablespoon Dijon-style
    mustard
1 tablespoon snipped parsley

● In a medium skillet cook apples in *2 tablespoons* of the butter or margarine over medium-high heat about 1 minute or till lightly browned, turning apples once. Remove from heat.

● Place the fish in a baking dish large enough to hold them in a single layer. Add apples. Pour in enough apple juice or cider to *half-cover* the fish. Cover with foil. Bake in a 350° oven till fish is done (allow about 20 minutes for butterfish, or about 30 minutes for porgies or trout). Transfer fish and apples to a platter, reserving ¼ *cup* of the liquid. Cover the fish and apples to keep them warm while preparing the sauce.

● For sauce, in a small saucepan cook onion in the remaining butter or margarine till tender but not brown. Stir in flour. Add the reserved liquid, the milk, and mustard. Cook and stir over medium heat till thickened and bubbly. Cook and stir for 1 minute more. Stir in parsley. Pass sauce with fish. Serves 4.

# Oven-Poached Bluefish with Tomato Cream Sauce

*Our taste testers also enjoyed this basil-tomato sauce on butterfish.*

1 2- to 3-pound dressed
    bluefish
    Salt
    Pepper
¼ cup sliced green onion
¾ cup Fish Stock (see recipe,
    page 57) *or* water
¾ cup dry white wine
    Tomato Cream Sauce

● Place fish in a 17x12x2-inch baking pan. Sprinkle fish with salt and pepper, then sprinkle with green onion. Pour in Fish Stock or water, then wine. Cover with foil. Bake in a 350° oven about 35 minutes or till the fish is done. Meanwhile, prepare the Tomato Cream Sauce. Pass sauce with fish. Serves 4 to 6.

**Tomato Cream Sauce:** In a medium saucepan combine one 14½-ounce can undrained *tomatoes,* cut up; ¼ cup thinly sliced *green onion;* ½ teaspoon *sugar;* ½ teaspoon dried *basil,* crushed; and ⅛ teaspoon *salt.* Bring to boiling, then reduce heat. Simmer, uncovered, for 5 minutes. Combine ½ cup *milk* and 1 tablespoon *cornstarch.* Add it to tomato mixture. Cook and stir over medium heat till thickened and bubbly. Cook and stir for 2 minutes more. Makes 2 cups.

# Waldorf-Style Stuffed Pike

1 cup chopped apple
½ cup thinly sliced celery
1 tablespoon butter *or* margarine
¼ cup mayonnaise *or* salad dressing
¼ cup chopped walnuts
2 teaspoons lemon juice
1 cup herb-seasoned stuffing mix
1 2-pound dressed pike, haddock, *or* red snapper
Cooking oil

● For stuffing, in a medium skillet cook apple and celery in butter or margarine till celery is tender. Remove from heat. Stir in mayonnaise or salad dressing, walnuts, and lemon juice. Add stuffing mix and toss till well mixed.

● To stuff fish, fill the cavity with stuffing, lightly patting the stuffing to flatten evenly. Tie fish closed. Place stuffed fish in a greased 12x7½x2-inch baking dish. Brush outside of fish with cooking oil. Cover loosely with foil. Bake in a 350° oven about 40 minutes or till fish is done. Makes 4 servings.

**To micro-cook:** Prepare Waldorf-Style Stuffed Pike as above, *except* in a 1-quart microwave-safe bowl combine apple, celery, and butter. Cover with vented clear plastic wrap. Micro-cook on 100% power (high) for 2 to 3 minutes or till celery is tender. Stir in mayonnaise or salad dressing, walnuts, lemon juice, and stuffing mix. Stuff fish. Cover dish with vented clear plastic wrap. Cook on high for 5 minutes. Rotate dish a half-turn; cook on high, covered, for 6 to 8 minutes more or till done.

# Baked Corn-Stuffed Fish

*Red snapper, pike, and whitefish are all good choices for this corny corn bread stuffing.*

1 10-ounce package corn bread mix
3 slices bacon
½ cup chopped onion
½ cup chopped celery
1 8¾-ounce can whole kernel corn
1 beaten egg
1 tablespoon snipped parsley
½ teaspoon ground sage
Dash salt
3 slices white bread, toasted and cut into cubes (about 2¼ cups)
1 3- to 4-pound dressed fish (see charts, pages 88–91)
2 tablespoons butter *or* margarine, melted

● Prepare corn bread mix according to package directions. Cool corn bread, then coarsely crumble enough of it to make *2 cups.* (Reserve the remaining corn bread for another use.)

● In a skillet cook bacon till crisp. Remove bacon and crumble. Set bacon aside. Cook onion and celery in bacon drippings till tender but not brown. Remove from heat.

● For stuffing, drain the corn, reserving liquid. In a medium mixing bowl combine corn, bacon, onion mixture, egg, parsley, sage, and salt. Add crumbled corn bread and bread cubes. Toss lightly till well mixed. Add enough of the reserved corn liquid to moisten (2 to 4 tablespoons), tossing gently to mix.

● To stuff fish, brush cavity with *half* of the butter or margarine. Fill fish cavity with stuffing, lightly patting stuffing to flatten evenly. (If all of the stuffing does not fit into fish, place remaining stuffing in a covered casserole and bake the last 25 minutes.) Tie or skewer fish closed. Place stuffed fish in a greased large shallow baking pan. Brush outside of fish with remaining butter or margarine. Cover loosely with foil. Bake in a 350° oven for 50 to 60 minutes or till fish is done. Serves 6 to 8.

# Tabbouleh-Stuffed Whitefish

1   cup boiling water
½   cup bulgur
⅓   cup finely chopped seeded
      cucumber
¼   cup snipped parsley
1   green onion, sliced
1   tablespoon snipped fresh
      mint *or* 1 teaspoon dried
      mint, crushed
1   tablespoon lemon juice
1   tablespoon cooking oil
½   teaspoon salt
1   2- to 2½-pound scaled
      drawn whitefish, lake
      trout, *or* red snapper
    Nonstick spray coating

● For stuffing, in a mixing bowl combine boiling water and bulgur. Let stand for 20 minutes. Drain well, then squeeze out excess water. Stir in cucumber, parsley, onion, mint, lemon juice, oil, and salt.

● To stuff fish, fill fish cavity with stuffing, lightly patting the stuffing to flatten evenly. (If all of the stuffing does not fit into fish, place remaining stuffing in a covered casserole and bake the last 25 minutes.) Tie or skewer fish closed.

● Spray a large shallow baking pan with nonstick coating. Place stuffed fish in the pan. Cover loosely with foil. Bake in a 350° oven about 40 minutes or till done. Makes 4 servings.

*Per serving:* 282 calories, 23 g protein, 334 mg sodium, 14 g fat, and 54 mg cholesterol.

# Swordfish and Fruit Kabobs

1   pound swordfish, sea bass,
      shark, *or* tuna steaks,
      cut 1 inch thick
¼   cup orange juice *and* 4 fresh
      plums, *or* one 15¼-ounce
      can pineapple chunks
      (juice pack)
2   tablespoons finely chopped
      onion
2   tablespoons dry sherry
2   tablespoons cooking oil
1   tablespoon sesame seed,
      toasted and crushed
1   clove garlic, minced
¼   teaspoon salt
⅛   teaspoon pepper
1   medium orange, cut into
      chunks
8   green onions, cut into 1½-
      inch pieces
    Nonstick spray coating

● Remove skin and bones from fish. Cut fish into 1-inch pieces. Place in a plastic bag, then set bag in a bowl. If using pineapple, drain it, reserving ¼ cup juice. For marinade, combine orange juice or reserved pineapple juice, chopped onion, sherry, oil, sesame seed, garlic, salt, and pepper. Pour over fish. Close bag and refrigerate for 4 to 6 hours, turning bag occasionally.

● For kabobs, drain fish, reserving the marinade. If using plums, pit and cut them into quarters. Using 8 long skewers, alternately thread fish, plums or pineapple, orange chunks, and green onions, leaving about ¼ inch of space between pieces.

● Spray the *cold* rack of an unheated broiler pan with nonstick coating. Place kabobs on the rack. Brush with some marinade. Broil 4 inches from the heat for 5 minutes. Turn kabobs over. Brush with marinade. Broil about 4 minutes more or till fish is done. Brush with more marinade before serving. Serves 4.

**To grill:** Prepare Swordfish and Fruit Kabobs as above, *except* spray the *cold* grill rack with nonstick coating. Place kabobs on rack. Grill, uncovered, directly over *medium-hot* coals for 8 to 12 minutes or till done. Turn and brush often with marinade.

*Per serving:* 267 calories, 23 g protein, 250 mg sodium, 12 g fat, and 55 mg cholesterol.

Swordfish and Fruit Kabobs

# Cusk and Garlic Bread Kabobs

*A nickname for cusk is "ocean catfish." Its flavor is so delicate that the garlic butter with a touch of red pepper adds a nice accent.*

12  fresh *or* frozen brussels
       sprouts, thawed
  4  medium carrots, cut into
       1½-inch pieces
  1  pound cusk *or* monkfish
       fillets, *or* swordfish
       steaks
16  1½-inch French bread cubes
  ½  cup butter *or* margarine,
       melted
  1  tablespoon snipped parsley
  ½  teaspoon garlic powder
       Dash ground red pepper

● Cut any large brussels sprouts in half. In a covered saucepan cook carrots in a small amount of boiling water for 3 minutes. Add brussels sprouts. Return to boiling; reduce heat. Cook, covered, about 7 minutes more or till nearly tender. Drain.

● Measure thickness of fish. Remove skin and bones from fish. Cut fish into 1-inch pieces. For fish kabobs, use 2 long skewers or 4 short skewers and alternately thread brussels sprouts, carrots, and fish, leaving about ¼ inch of space between pieces.

● For bread kabobs, use 2 long or 4 short skewers and thread bread cubes, leaving about ½ inch of space between pieces. Combine butter or margarine, parsley, garlic, and pepper.

● Place fish and bread kabobs on an ungreased rack of an unheated broiler pan. Brush with *half* of the butter mixture. Broil 4 inches from the heat till fish is done and bread is toasted, turning kabobs over once during broiling. (Allow 4 to 6 minutes per ½-inch thickness of fish.) Brush kabobs with the remaining butter mixture before serving. Makes 4 servings.

**To grill:** Prepare the Cusk and Garlic Bread Kabobs as above, *except* brush grill rack with *cooking oil.* Grill kabobs on an uncovered grill directly over *medium-hot* coals till fish is done and bread is toasted, turning kabobs over once and brushing with butter. (Allow 4 to 6 minutes per ½-inch thickness of fish.)

## Lighting the Briquettes

Grilling foods to perfection is easy to do if you know all the rules.
● To start the fire, pile the briquettes into a pyramid shape in the center of the firebox. Squirt the briquettes with a starter fluid, then wait for 1 minute and light the briquettes.
● When the briquettes look ash gray, spread the coals in a single layer for direct cooking. For indirect cooking, arrange the coals in a circle around the edge of the firebox, leaving the center open.
● Test the coals for hotness by holding your hand over the center. Then start counting the seconds. If you need to remove your hand after three seconds, the coals are *medium-hot.* If it takes four seconds, the coals are *medium.*

# Herb-Marinated Grouper

*Good 'n' herby with just a hint of hotness.*

10 ounces skinless grouper
    fillets *or* steaks
½ cup dry white wine
2 tablespoons olive oil *or*
    cooking oil
1 green onion, sliced
1 small clove garlic, minced
½ teaspoon dried basil,
    crushed
¼ teaspoon salt
¼ teaspoon dried oregano,
    crushed
⅛ teaspoon crushed red
    pepper

● Measure thickness of fish. Place fish in a baking dish large enough to hold the fish in a single layer.

● For marinade, combine wine, oil, onion, garlic, basil, salt, oregano, and red pepper. Pour over fish. Turn fish to coat it with marinade. Cover and marinate fish in the refrigerator for 4 to 6 hours, turning fish over occasionally.

● Drain fish, reserving marinade. Place fish on a greased rack of an unheated broiler pan. Brush fish with some of the reserved marinade. Broil 4 inches from the heat till the fish is done, brushing occasionally with the marinade. (Allow 4 to 6 minutes per ½-inch thickness of fish.) If fish is 1 inch or more thick, carefully turn it over halfway through broiling. Serves 2.

**To grill:** Prepare Herb-Marinated Grouper as above, *except* place fish in a well-greased wire grill basket. Brush with marinade, then close basket. Grill on an uncovered grill directly over *medium-hot* coals till done, brushing occasionally with marinade. (Allow 4 to 6 minutes per ½-inch thickness of fish.) If fish is 1 inch or more thick, turn it over halfway through grilling.

# Teriyaki Halibut

*When you're grilling a flaky fish like halibut, use a wire grill basket for easy turning.*

2 halibut, shark, *or* tuna
    steaks, cut 1 inch thick
    (about 1 pound)
¼ cup soy sauce
2 tablespoons sake *or* dry
    sherry
1 tablespoon sugar
1 teaspoon dry mustard
1 teaspoon grated gingerroot
2 cloves garlic, minced

● Place fish in a baking dish large enough to hold the fish in a single layer. For the marinade, combine soy sauce, sake or dry sherry, sugar, mustard, gingerroot, and garlic. Pour over fish. Turn fish to coat it with marinade. Cover and marinate fish in the refrigerator for 4 to 6 hours, turning fish over occasionally.

● Drain fish, reserving marinade. Place fish on a greased rack of an unheated broiler pan. Brush fish with some of the reserved marinade. Broil 4 inches from the heat for 5 minutes. Using a wide spatula, carefully turn fish over. Brush with more of the marinade and broil for 3 to 7 minutes more or till fish is done. Brush with marinade before serving. Makes 2 servings.

**To grill:** Prepare Teriyaki Halibut as directed above, *except* brush grill rack with *cooking oil*. Place fish on rack. Brush fish with marinade. Grill fish on an uncovered grill directly over *medium-hot* coals for 5 minutes. Carefully turn fish over. Brush with more marinade and grill for 3 to 7 minutes more or till fish is done. Brush with marinade before serving.

Basil-Buttered Steaks
(grilled version)

# Sesame-Dill Shark

*Toasted sesame seed not only adds a nutty flavor, but garnishes the steaks, too.*

3 shark, halibut, salmon, *or* swordfish steaks, cut 1 inch thick (about 1½ pounds)
2 teaspoons finely shredded lemon peel
¼ cup lemon juice
2 tablespoons cooking oil
1 teaspoon dried dillweed
2 teaspoons sesame seed, toasted

● Place fish in a baking dish large enough to hold the fish in a single layer. For the marinade, combine lemon peel, lemon juice, cooking oil, and dillweed. Pour over fish. Turn fish to coat it with marinade. Cover and marinate fish in the refrigerator for 4 to 6 hours, turning fish over occasionally.

● Drain the fish, reserving the marinade. Place fish on a greased rack of an unheated broiler pan. Brush with some reserved marinade. Broil 4 inches from the heat for 5 minutes. Using a wide spatula, carefully turn the fish over. Brush with more marinade. Broil for 3 to 7 minutes more or till fish is done.

● To serve, brush with marinade and sprinkle with toasted sesame seed. Makes 3 servings.

**To grill:** Prepare Sesame-Dill Shark as directed above, *except* brush grill rack with *cooking oil.* Place fish on rack. Brush fish with marinade. Grill fish on an uncovered grill directly over *medium-hot* coals for 5 minutes. Carefully turn fish over. Brush with more marinade and grill for 3 to 7 minutes more or till fish is done. Brush with marinade and sprinkle with sesame seed.

# Basil-Buttered Steaks

*"The simpler, the better" describes these grilled steaks topped with an herb butter.*

½ cup butter *or* margarine, softened
1 tablespoon snipped fresh basil *or* 1 teaspoon dried basil, crushed
1 tablespoon snipped parsley
2 teaspoons lemon juice
4 halibut, salmon, shark, *or* swordfish steaks, cut 1 inch thick (about 2 pounds)

● For butter mixture, in a small mixing bowl combine butter or margarine, basil, parsley, and lemon juice. Mix till well blended.

● Place the fish on a greased rack of an unheated broiler pan. Lightly brush fish with some of the butter mixture. Broil 4 inches from the heat for 5 minutes. Then, using a wide spatula, carefully turn fish over. Lightly brush with more of the butter mixture. Broil for 3 to 7 minutes more or till fish is done.

● To serve, dollop remaining butter mixture on top of fish. Makes 4 servings.

**To grill:** Prepare Basil-Buttered Steaks as directed above, *except* brush grill rack with *cooking oil.* Place fish on rack. Lightly brush fish with butter mixture. Grill fish on an uncovered grill directly over *medium-hot* coals for 5 minutes. Carefully turn fish over. Lightly brush with more butter mixture and grill for 3 to 7 minutes more or till fish is done. Dollop remaining butter mixture on top of fish.

# Gingered Plum-Glazed Halibut

*Just one bite and you're off to the Orient! The sweet 'n' sour glaze, with its touch of hotness, is what sends you on your way.*

¾ cup red plum jam
1 tablespoon vinegar
½ teaspoon grated gingerroot
   *or* ⅛ teaspoon ground
   ginger
½ teaspoon crushed red
   pepper
⅛ teaspoon garlic powder
4 halibut, shark, *or* swordfish
   steaks, cut 1 inch thick
   (about 2 pounds)
   Cooking oil

● For glaze, in a small saucepan combine plum jam, vinegar, gingerroot, red pepper, and garlic powder. Bring mixture to boiling, stirring constantly. Then remove from heat.

● Place the fish on a greased rack of an unheated broiler pan. Lightly brush fish with cooking oil. Broil 4 inches from the heat for 5 minutes. Using a wide spatula, carefully turn fish over. Lightly brush fish with more cooking oil. Broil for 3 to 7 minutes more or till done, brushing fish with some of the glaze the last 2 minutes of broiling. Pass the remaining glaze. Serves 4.

**To grill:** Prepare the Gingered-Plum-Glazed Halibut as directed above, *except* brush grill rack with cooking oil. Place fish on rack. Lightly brush fish with cooking oil. Grill on an uncovered grill directly over *medium-hot* coals for 5 minutes. Carefully turn fish over and lightly brush with more cooking oil. Grill for 3 to 7 minutes more or till done, brushing fish with some of the glaze the last 2 minutes. Pass remaining glaze.

# Orange-Cumin Tuna

Light & LOW

*Orange twists and parsley dress up these glistening steaks.*

2 teaspoons cornstarch
1 teaspoon brown sugar
⅛ teaspoon ground cumin
   Dash salt
¾ cup orange juice
   Nonstick spray coating
4 tuna *or* swordfish steaks,
   cut ½ inch thick (about
   1 pound)
1 tablespoon olive oil *or*
   cooking oil
   Orange slices (optional)
   Parsley sprigs (optional)

● For sauce, in a small saucepan combine cornstarch, sugar, cumin, and salt. Stir in orange juice. Cook and stir till thickened and bubbly. Cook and stir for 2 minutes more. Remove from heat. Cover to keep warm while cooking fish.

● Spray the *cold* rack of an unheated broiler pan with nonstick coating. Place fish on the rack. Brush fish with the oil. Broil 4 inches from the heat for 4 to 6 minutes or till fish is done.

● To serve, transfer fish to a platter. Spoon sauce over fish. If desired, garnish with orange twists and parsley. Serves 4.

**To grill:** Prepare Orange-Cumin Tuna as directed above, *except* spray the *cold* grill rack with nonstick coating. Place fish on rack. Brush fish with the oil. Grill on an uncovered grill directly over *medium-hot* coals for 4 to 6 minutes or till fish is done. Serve as above.

*Per serving:* 239 calories, 28 g protein, 100 mg sodium, 10 g fat, and 43 mg cholesterol.

# Five-Spice Smoked Fish

*Turn your full-size grill into a smoker.*

2 cups applewood *or* Osage
    orangewood chips, *or* 4 to
    6 mesquite chunks
1 3- to 4-pound dressed cod,
    pollack, red snapper,
    sea bass, *or* sea trout
1 teaspoon ground cinnamon
1 teaspoon aniseed, crushed,
    *or* 1 star anise, crushed
½ teaspoon salt
¼ teaspoon fennel seed,
    crushed
¼ teaspoon coarse ground
    pepper *or* Szechuan
    pepper
⅛ teaspoon ground cloves
1 tablespoon cooking oil

● At least 1 hour before smoke-cooking, soak the wood in enough *water* to cover. Meanwhile, using a sharp knife, cut ½-inch-deep diagonal slits, 1 inch apart, into both sides of fish.

● For the seasoning mixture, combine cinnamon, aniseed, salt, fennel seed, pepper, and cloves. Rub fish cavity with some of the seasoning mixture. Rub oil into slits. Then rub the remaining seasonings on outside of fish, pressing seasonings into the slits.

● Tear off a piece of *heavy* foil large enough to hold fish. Prick a few holes in the foil. Drain the wood. To smoke-cook the fish, in a covered grill arrange preheated coals around a foil drip pan. (The fish is too large to fit in a water smoker.) Test for *medium* heat above the pan. Place the drained wood on the preheated coals. Place fish on foil on the rack over center of drip pan, but not over coals. Lower grill hood. Grill for 40 to 50 minutes or till fish is done. Makes 6 to 8 servings.

*Per serving:* 231 calories, 38 g protein, 360 mg sodium, 7 g fat, and 76 mg cholesterol.

### Preparing the fish
Use a dressed fish or remove the head and tail from a drawn fish. Otherwise, the fish will be too large to fit on the grill rack.

    Cut ½-inch-deep diagonal slits about 1 inch apart on both sides of the fish. During smoke-cooking, the fish will absorb the blend of the spices through these slits.

# Smoked Trout with Horseradish Sauce

4 to 6 mesquite chunks
2 8- to 10-ounce scaled drawn
  rainbow trout, coho
  salmon, *or* porgies, *or*
  12 ounces salmon *or*
  mackerel fillets (about
  ½ inch thick)
  Cooking oil
  Horseradish Sauce

● At least 1 hour before smoke-cooking, soak wood in enough *water* to cover. Lightly brush outside and cavity of drawn fish (or both sides of fillets) with oil. Tear off a piece of *heavy* foil large enough to hold fish in a single layer. Prick a few holes into foil. Drain wood. Use one of the following methods to smoke-cook the fish. Pass sauce with fish. Makes 2 or 3 servings.

● *Grill method:* In a covered grill arrange preheated coals around a foil drip pan. Test for *medium* heat above pan. Pour about 1 inch of *water* into the pan. Place wood on the preheated coals. Place fish on foil on the grill rack over drip pan, but not over coals. Lower hood. Grill for 20 to 25 minutes or till done.

● *Smoker method:* In a water smoker arrange preheated coals, wood chunks, and water pan according to the manufacturer's directions. Pour *water* into pan. Place fish on foil on the rack over pan. Lower hood. Grill for 20 to 25 minutes or till done.

**Horseradish Sauce:** Whip ½ cup *whipping cream* till soft peaks form. Then fold in 2 teaspoons prepared *horseradish* and 1 teaspoon *tarragon vinegar.* Cover and chill for up to 1 hour. Makes about 1 cup.

# Spicy-Hot Fillets

⅓ cup all-purpose flour
2 tablespoons cornmeal
1 teaspoon chili powder
½ to 1 teaspoon ground red
  pepper
½ teaspoon garlic powder
½ teaspoon paprika
1½ pounds firm-textured fillets
  (½ to 1 inch thick) (see
  charts, pages 88–91)
2 tablespoons butter *or*
  margarine
2 tablespoons cooking oil

● In a shallow dish combine flour, cornmeal, chili powder, red pepper, garlic powder, paprika, 1½ teaspoons *salt,* and ⅛ teaspoon *pepper.* Dip fish into flour mixture.

● In a large skillet heat *half* of the butter or margarine and *half* of the oil. Add *half* of the fish to the skillet in a single layer. Fry over medium heat till fish is done and coating is golden brown, turning once (allow 3 to 8 minutes total). Remove fish from skillet and drain on paper towels. Repeat with remaining butter or margarine, oil, and fish. Makes 6 servings.

Spicy-Hot Fillets

# Crispy Pan-Fried Lake Fish

*Going fishing? Carry the dry ingredients in a plastic bag for a quick shore lunch.*

½ cup finely crushed saltine crackers (14 crackers) *or* cornflakes *or* fine dry bread crumbs
¼ cup grated Parmesan cheese
1 tablespoon snipped parsley
¼ teaspoon lemon pepper
1 beaten egg
4 8- to 10-ounce dressed lake perch, rainbow trout, *or* other dressed fish, *or* 1 pound firm-textured fillets (½ to ¾ inch thick) (see charts, pages 88–91)
3 to 4 tablespoons shortening *or* cooking oil
Lemon slices, halved (optional)
Fresh parsley, rosemary, *or* dill (optional)

● In a shallow dish combine crackers, cornflakes, or bread crumbs; Parmesan cheese; 1 tablespoon parsley; and lemon pepper. In another shallow dish place egg. Dip fish into egg, then roll fish in the crumb mixture.

● In a large skillet heat *half* of the shortening or cooking oil. (If necessary, add more shortening or oil during frying.) Add *half* of the fish to the skillet in a single layer. Fry over medium heat till fish is done and coating is golden brown, turning once (allow 8 to 12 minutes total for dressed fish or 3 to 6 minutes total for fillets). Remove fish from skillet and drain on paper towels. Repeat with remaining shortening or oil and fish. Season fish to taste with *salt* and *pepper*. If desired, serve fish with lemon and garnish with additional parsley, rosemary, or dill. Serves 4.

# Sweet 'n' Sour Stir-Fry

*A colorful dish with an Oriental flair.*

1 pound skinless cusk, orange roughy, red snapper, *or* whiting fillets (½ to 1 inch thick)
1 8-ounce can pineapple tidbits (juice pack)
¼ cup packed brown sugar
¼ cup cider vinegar
2 tablespoons cornstarch
1 tablespoon soy sauce
1 teaspoon garlic salt
1 teaspoon ground ginger
1 tablespoon cooking oil
1 small green pepper, cut into ¾-inch pieces
1 8-ounce can sliced water chestnuts, drained
2 tablespoons diced pimiento
2 cups hot cooked rice

● Cut fish into 1-inch pieces. Cover and refrigerate the fish till needed. Drain pineapple, reserving juice. Set pineapple aside.

● For sauce, add enough *water* to juice to make *1⅓ cups*. Stir in sugar, vinegar, cornstarch, soy sauce, garlic salt, and ginger.

● Preheat a wok or large skillet over medium-high heat; add oil. (If necessary, add more oil during stir-frying.) Stir-fry green pepper and water chestnuts about 2 minutes or till the green pepper is nearly tender. Remove vegetables from wok. Add *half* of the fish to the hot wok. Stir-fry for 3 to 6 minutes or till done, being careful not to break up pieces. Gently remove fish from wok. Repeat with remaining fish, then remove it from wok.

● Stir sauce, then add it to the wok. Cook and stir till thickened and bubbly. Cook and stir for 1 minute more. Return vegetables and fish to wok, then add pineapple and pimiento. Toss lightly to coat. Reduce heat. Cover and cook for 1 minute more. Serve over hot cooked rice. Makes 4 servings.

# Dilled Pike and Pea Pods

*You won't be cheating on your diet with this creamy, rich-tasting dish.*

8 ounces skinless pike fillets,
   *or* halibut *or* shark steaks
   (½ to 1 inch thick)
2 teaspoons all-purpose flour
⅓ cup plain yogurt
¼ cup milk
1 teaspoon instant chicken
   bouillon granules
¾ teaspoon snipped dill *or* ¼
   teaspoon dried dillweed
   Nonstick spray coating
1 medium carrot, thinly bias
   sliced
1 cup fresh pea pods *or* ½ of a
   6-ounce package frozen
   pea pods, thawed
1 tablespoon cooking oil

● If using fish steaks, remove skin and bones. Cut fish into 1-inch pieces. Cover and refrigerate till needed.

● For sauce, in a small mixing bowl stir flour into yogurt, then stir in milk, bouillon granules, and dill. Set sauce aside.

● Spray a *cold* wok or large skillet with the nonstick coating. Preheat wok or skillet over medium-high heat. Stir-fry carrot for 2 minutes. Add pea pods and stir-fry for 2 to 3 minutes more or till nearly tender. Remove vegetables from the wok. Add oil to wok. Stir-fry fish for 3 to 6 minutes or till fish is done, being careful not to break up pieces. Gently remove fish from wok.

● Reduce heat, then add sauce to the wok. Cook and stir till thickened and bubbly. Cook and stir for 1 minute more. Return vegetables and fish to wok. Toss lightly to coat, then heat through. Makes 2 servings.

*Per serving:* 269 calories, 28 g protein, 318 mg sodium, 11 g fat, and 43 mg cholesterol.

**Stir-frying the fish**
After you've cooked the vegetables, stir-fry the fish. Begin by adding the fish to the hot wok. Using a spatula or long-handled spoon, *gently* lift and turn the pieces with a folding motion so the fish cooks evenly. The fish will be done when it's opaque and flakes easily with a fork.

   Remember to keep the pieces moving at all times to prevent scorching. And be sure to lift the fish *gently* so that it doesn't break up.

# Fish Stroganoff

1 pound swordfish *or* tuna
  steaks, *or* skinless cusk
  *or* mahimahi fillets
  (about 1 inch thick)
1½ cups sliced fresh
  mushrooms
½ cup chopped onion
1 clove garlic, minced
¼ cup butter *or* margarine
3 tablespoons all-purpose
  flour
1 tablespoon tomato paste
1 teaspoon instant chicken
  bouillon granules
½ teaspoon dried basil,
  crushed
2 tablespoons dry white wine
1 8-ounce carton dairy
  sour cream
  Hot cooked noodles

● If using steaks, remove skin and bones. Cut fish into 1-inch pieces. In a large skillet cook mushrooms, onion, and garlic in *half* of the butter or margarine about 4 minutes or till onion is tender. Using a slotted spoon, remove vegetables from skillet. Add fish to skillet. Fry over medium-high heat for 4 to 6 minutes or till done, gently lifting and turning fish occasionally but being careful not to break up pieces. Remove fish from skillet.

● For sauce, melt remaining butter or margarine in the skillet. Stir in *1 tablespoon* of the flour, tomato paste, chicken bouillon granules, basil, and ¼ teaspoon *salt*. Then stir in 1¼ cups *water*. Cook and stir mixture over medium heat till thickened and bubbly. Cook and stir for 1 minute more.

● Stir remaining flour and the wine into sour cream. Then stir it into the mixture in skillet. Cook and stir till thickened and bubbly. Return mushroom mixture and fish to skillet. Toss lightly to coat. Cook and gently turn mixture till heated through. Serve over cooked noodles. If desired, sprinkle with snipped parsley. Makes 4 servings.

# Fish 'n' Chips

*Light, crispy, and crunchy. Use the beer batter on mild-flavored fillets such as cod or orange roughy. Or try it on smelt and have a smelt-fry party.*

1 pound skinless firm-
  textured lean fillets (about
  ½ inch thick) (see charts,
  pages 88–91) *or* dressed
  smelt
1 pound medium potatoes
  (about 3)
  Shortening *or* cooking oil for
  deep-fat frying
1 cup all-purpose flour
1 cup beer
1 egg
½ teaspoon baking powder
¼ teaspoon salt
  Tartar Sauce (see recipe,
  page 52) (optional)
  Malt vinegar *or* cider vinegar
  (optional)
  Coarse salt (optional)

● Cut fillets into about 3x2-inch pieces. If necessary, pat fish dry with paper towels. Cover and refrigerate till needed.

● For chips, cut the potatoes lengthwise into about ⅜-inch-wide strips. Pat dry with paper towels. In a 3-quart saucepan or deep-fat fryer heat 2 inches of shortening or cooking oil to 375°. Fry potatoes, ¼ at a time, for 4 to 6 minutes or till *lightly* browned. Remove potatoes and drain on paper towels. Transfer potatoes to a wire rack on a baking sheet. Spread potatoes into a single layer. Keep warm in a 300° oven while frying fish.

● Meanwhile, for batter, in a medium mixing bowl combine flour, beer, egg, baking powder, and salt. Beat with a rotary beater or wire whisk till smooth. Dip fish into batter. Then fry in the hot fat (375°) till done and coating is golden brown, turning once (allow 3 to 4 minutes total for fillets, 1 to 1½ minutes total for smelt). Remove fish and drain on paper towels. Transfer fish to another baking sheet. Keep it warm in the oven till all of fish is fried. If desired, serve Tartar Sauce for dipping or vinegar and coarse salt to sprinkle on top of fish and chips. Serves 4.

**Tartar Sauce**
(see recipe, page 52)

Fish 'n' Chips

# Tuna-Potato Cakes

*Turn a meat 'n' potato lover into a fish 'n' potato lover with these golden little patties.*

1 medium potato, peeled and
   quartered
8 ounces cooked tuna,
   mackerel, pike, *or* salmon
   (see tip, page 10)
1 beaten egg
2 tablespoons grated onion
1 tablespoon snipped parsley
1 teaspoon lemon juice
½ teaspoon garlic salt
⅛ teaspoon pepper
1 beaten egg
1 tablespoon milk
¾ cup fine dry seasoned bread
   crumbs
2 tablespoons grated
   Parmesan cheese
2 tablespoons cooking oil
   Tartar Sauce *or* Green
   Chili Salsa (see recipes,
   pages 52 or 53)

● In a small covered saucepan cook potato in boiling salted water about 15 minutes or till tender, then drain. In a medium mixing bowl mash the potato. (You should have about ¾ cup.)

● Flake the fish. (You should have about 1½ cups.) Stir fish, 1 beaten egg, onion, parsley, lemon juice, garlic salt, and pepper into the mashed potato in the bowl. Shape mixture into eight ¾-inch-thick patties. Cover and chill about 30 minutes.

● In a shallow dish combine 1 beaten egg and milk. In another shallow dish combine bread crumbs and Parmesan cheese. Dip fish patties into egg mixture, then into crumb mixture.

● In a medium skillet heat oil. (If necessary, add more oil during frying.) Add the patties to the skillet in a single layer. Fry over medium heat till golden brown, turning once (allow about 6 minutes total). Serve patties with sauce. Makes 4 servings.

# Fish and Crabmeat Patties

*Keep cooked patties piping hot in a 325° oven while frying the remaining patties.*

12 ounces cooked Atlantic
   ocean perch, cod,
   flounder, *or* pike
   (see tip, page 10)
1 6-ounce package frozen
   crabmeat, thawed, well
   drained, and flaked
⅓ cup fine dry bread crumbs
2 beaten eggs
2 green onions, sliced
1 teaspoon finely shredded
   lemon peel
1 teaspoon lemon juice
½ teaspoon salt
⅛ teaspoon pepper
½ cup fine dry bread crumbs
2 tablespoons cooking oil

● Flake the fish. (You should have about 2¼ cups.) For patties, in a medium mixing bowl combine the fish, crab, ⅓ cup bread crumbs, eggs, onions, lemon peel, lemon juice, salt, and pepper. Shape the mixture into eight ¾-inch-thick patties. Cover and chill about 30 minutes.

● In a shallow dish place ½ cup bread crumbs. Dip patties into crumbs. In a large skillet heat *half* of the oil. (If necessary, add more oil during frying.) Add *half* of the patties to the skillet in a single layer. Fry over medium heat till golden brown, turning once (allow about 6 minutes total). Remove patties from the skillet. Repeat with remaining oil and patties.

● To serve, arrange the fried patties on a lettuce-lined serving platter and garnish with lemon wedges or slices, if desired. Makes 4 servings.

# Fish Foo Yong

*Fish Foo Yong, Fish Foo Yong, Fish Foo Yong—now say that FAST three times! Whether you can or can't, you'll want to savor every bite slowly.*

½ cup finely chopped Chinese cabbage *or* cabbage
¼ cup chopped onion
¼ cup chopped green pepper
3 tablespoons cooking oil
1 tablespoon cornstarch
1 teaspoon instant chicken bouillon granules
½ teaspoon grated gingerroot *or* ¼ teaspoon ground ginger
1 cup cold water
1 tablespoon soy sauce
1 teaspoon molasses
6 ounces skinless firm-textured lean fillets (see charts, pages 88–91)
3 beaten eggs
¼ teaspoon salt
⅛ teaspoon pepper
1 cup coarsely chopped fresh *or* canned bean sprouts

● In a large skillet cook cabbage, onion, and green pepper in *1 tablespoon* of the cooking oil about 2 minutes or till nearly tender. Remove from heat and cool slightly.

● Meanwhile, for the sauce, in a small saucepan combine the cornstarch, bouillon granules, and gingerroot. Stir in water, soy sauce, and molasses. Cook and stir mixture over medium heat till thickened and bubbly. Cook and stir it for 2 minutes more. Remove from heat. Cover to keep warm while frying patties.

● For egg mixture, finely chop raw fish. (You should have about ¾ cup.) In a medium mixing bowl beat together eggs, salt, and pepper. Stir in raw fish, cabbage mixture, and bean sprouts.

● In the large skillet heat *1 tablespoon* of the cooking oil. (If necessary, add more oil during frying.) For each patty, stir the egg mixture, then use about ¼ *cup* of it. Make 3 or 4 patties in the skillet, spreading the vegetables and fish so that they cover the egg as it spreads. Fry over medium heat till golden, turning once (allow about 3 minutes total). Remove from skillet and cover to keep warm. Repeat with remaining oil and egg mixture. To serve, spoon warm sauce over patties. Makes 4 servings.

**Seafood Foo Yong:** Prepare the Fish Foo Yong as directed above, *except* use 3 ounces finely chopped raw *fish* and 3 ounces finely chopped raw *shrimp* instead of the 6 ounces raw fish. (You should have about ¾ cup total of fish and shrimp.)

# Monkfish with Grapes and Cashews

*Simple but elegant.*

1 pound skinless monkfish, mahimahi, *or* sea bass fillets (about 1 inch thick)
3 tablespoons butter *or* margarine
¾ cup seedless grapes, halved
½ cup cashews
½ teaspoon finely shredded orange peel
3 tablespoons orange juice

● Cut fish into 1-inch pieces. In a large skillet heat butter or margarine. Add fish to the skillet. Fry over medium-high heat for 4 to 6 minutes or till done, gently lifting and turning the fish occasionally but being careful not to break up pieces. Gently transfer to a heated platter. Cover to keep warm.

● In the same skillet add grapes, cashews, orange peel, and orange juice. Cook and stir till heated through. Spoon over fish. Makes 4 servings.

# Fish Marsala

*Just add steamed carrots and broccoli and you've got an attractive meal.*

1 pound skinless cod,
   grouper, pollack, *or*
   whiting fillets
   (¾ to 1 inch thick)
Nonstick spray coating
1½ cups sliced fresh
   mushrooms
3 green onions, sliced
¾ cup Fish Stock (see recipe,
   page 57) *or* chicken broth
¼ cup dry marsala *or* dry
   sherry

● Cut fillets lengthwise into 2½-inch-wide strips. Spray a *cold* medium skillet with nonstick coating. Add fish to the skillet in a single layer. Cook over medium heat till fish is done, turning once (allow 8 to 10 minutes total). Remove fish from skillet. Cover fish to keep warm while preparing sauce.

● For sauce, in the skillet cook mushrooms and green onions in *2 tablespoons* of the Fish Stock or chicken broth for 3 to 4 minutes or till tender. Remove vegetables from skillet; set aside.

● Add marsala or sherry and remaining stock or broth to the skillet. Bring mixture to boiling, then reduce heat. Boil gently, uncovered, about 6 minutes or till liquid is reduced to ⅓ cup. Stir in vegetables, then arrange fish on top. Cover and cook about 1 minute or till heated through. Makes 4 servings.

*Per serving:* 130 calories, 23 g protein, 205 mg sodium, 1 g fat, and 56 mg cholesterol.

# Salmon with Almonds and Pecans

*Also try the creamy buttery Beurre Blanc Sauce on vegetables or eggs.*

Beurre Blanc Sauce
1 pound skinless salmon
   fillets (¾ to 1 inch
   thick)
2 tablespoons all-purpose
   flour
1 tablespoon cooking oil
¼ cup water
⅓ cup sliced almonds, toasted,
   *or* coarsely chopped
   macadamia nuts, toasted
⅓ cup pecan halves

● Prepare Beurre Blanc Sauce and set aside. Cut fillets into 4 equal portions. Dip salmon pieces into flour, turning to coat.

● In a medium skillet heat oil. (If necessary, add more oil during frying.) Add fish to the skillet. Fry over medium heat till fish is done, turning once (allow 8 to 10 minutes total). Remove skillet from heat. Remove salmon from skillet; cover to keep warm.

● Add water to the skillet. Stir for 1 to 2 minutes, scraping up any brown bits from bottom of skillet. Add Beurre Blanc Sauce and return skillet to heat. Heat mixture through, but *do not boil.* Stir in nuts. Spoon mixture over salmon. Serves 4.

**Beurre Blanc Sauce:** In a small saucepan combine ¼ cup dry *white wine*, 2 tablespoons *white vinegar*, 2 tablespoons *water*, 2 tablespoons chopped *shallots or* sliced *green onion*, and dash *white pepper*. Bring to boiling, then reduce heat. Simmer, uncovered, for 8 to 10 minutes or till reduced to *half* (about ¼ cup). Remove from heat. Using a wire whisk, stir in ½ cup *butter or margarine*, 1 tablespoon at a time, till butter is melted. If desired, stir in 1 tablespoon snipped *chives*. Makes ¾ cup.

Orange-Pineapple Sauce

Citrus-Almond Sauce
(orange version)

# Sauces

*The eleven special sauces in this section are good on any kind of fish.*

## Hot Citrus Sauce

*Lemon or orange—what's your fancy? You pick the flavor of this sauce.*

½  cup chicken broth
¼  teaspoon finely shredded
    lemon *or* orange peel
4  teaspoons lemon *or* orange
    juice
2  teaspoons cornstarch
1  tablespoon butter *or*
    margarine

● In a small saucepan combine chicken broth, peel, juice, and cornstarch. Cook and stir over medium heat till thickened and bubbly. Cook and stir for 1 minute more. Remove from heat; stir in the butter or margarine. Serve immediately. Makes ½ cup.

**Citrus-Almond Sauce:** Prepare Hot Citrus Sauce as directed above. Stir in 2 tablespoons sliced *almonds*. Makes ½ cup.

**Lemon-Dill Sauce:** Prepare Hot Citrus Sauce as directed above, using lemon peel and juice. Stir in ⅛ teaspoon dried *dillweed* before cooking. Makes ½ cup.

**Orange-Pineapple Sauce:** Prepare Hot Citrus Sauce as directed above, using the orange peel and juice. Stir in 1 tablespoon unsweetened *pineapple juice* before cooking. Makes ½ cup.

Tartar Sauce

Creamy Tarragon Sauce

## Creamy Tarragon Sauce

*Have any leftover sauce? Cover and store it in the refrigerator for up to 10 days.*

1  1-ounce envelope
   hollandaise sauce mix
2  tablespoons dry white wine
½  teaspoon dried tarragon,
   crushed
½  cup mayonnaise *or* salad
   dressing

● In a small saucepan prepare sauce mix according to package directions. Remove from heat and stir in wine and tarragon. Let cool for 10 to 15 minutes.

● In a small mixing bowl fold the tarragon mixture into the mayonnaise or salad dressing. Serve sauce at room temperature. Makes 1¼ cups.

## Tartar Sauce

*An old standby you can mix in minutes.*

1  cup mayonnaise *or* salad
   dressing
¼  cup finely chopped dill
   pickle *or* sweet pickle
   relish
1  tablespoon finely chopped
   onion
1  tablespoon snipped parsley
1  tablespoon diced pimiento
1  teaspoon lemon juice

● In a small mixing bowl combine the mayonnaise or salad dressing, dill pickle or pickle relish, onion, parsley, pimiento, and lemon juice. Stir till well blended. If desired, cover and chill to blend the flavors before serving. Makes 1 cup.

Green Chili Salsa

Cucumber-Dill Sauce

# Cucumber-Dill Sauce

*It's tangy but so good!*

⅓ cup finely chopped, seeded, peeled cucumber
¼ cup plain yogurt
¼ cup reduced-calorie mayonnaise *or* salad dressing
2 tablespoons milk
¼ teaspoon dried dillweed

● In a small mixing bowl combine chopped cucumber, yogurt, mayonnaise or salad dressing, milk, and dillweed. Stir till well blended. If desired, cover and chill to blend the flavors before serving. Makes ¾ cup.

*Per 1 tablespoon serving:* 20 calories, 0 g protein, 33 mg sodium, 2 g fat, and 0 mg cholesterol.

# Green Chili Salsa

*If you like it hot, add the pepper sauce.*

1 14½-ounce can sodium-free tomatoes, drained
1 4-ounce can whole green chili peppers, drained
2 tablespoons chopped onion
1 clove garlic, minced
  Several dashes bottled hot pepper sauce (optional)

● In a blender container or food processor bowl place tomatoes, chili peppers, onion, garlic, and hot pepper sauce, if desired. Cover and blend or process about 5 seconds or till combined, but still chunky. Serve at room temperature, or transfer to a small saucepan and heat just till warm. Makes 1½ cups.

*Per 1 tablespoon serving:* 5 calories, 0 g protein, 3 mg sodium, 0 g fat, and 0 mg cholesterol.

Mustard-Caper Sauce

Blender Hollandaise Sauce

# Blender Hollandaise Sauce

*A tip from our Test Kitchen: Reheat this creamy rich sauce in a small saucepan over very low heat, stirring constantly.*

½  cup butter *or* margarine
2  tablespoons lemon juice
   Dash ground red pepper
3  egg yolks

● In a saucepan heat butter or margarine, lemon juice, and red pepper till butter is melted and the mixture is almost boiling. Remove from heat.

● Place egg yolks in a blender container. Cover and blend for 5 seconds. Through the opening in the lid or with lid ajar, and with blender on high speed, *gradually* add butter mixture. Blend about 30 seconds more or till thick and fluffy, stopping to scrape sides as needed. Serve immediately. Makes 1 cup.

# Mustard-Caper Sauce

1  tablespoon butter *or* margarine
1  tablespoon all-purpose flour
⅛  teaspoon salt
   Dash white pepper
1  cup milk
2  tablespoons Dijon-style mustard
1  tablespoon capers, drained

● In a small saucepan melt butter or margarine. Stir in flour, salt, and pepper. Then add milk. Cook and stir over medium heat till thickened and bubbly. Cook and stir for 1 minute more. Remove from heat; stir in mustard and capers. Makes ¾ cup.

**Mornay Sauce:** Prepare Mustard-Caper Sauce as directed above, *except* omit mustard and capers. Stir ¼ cup shredded *Gruyère or* process *Swiss cheese* (1 ounce) and 2 tablespoons grated *Parmesan cheese* into the cooked sauce till shredded cheese melts. Makes 1 cup.

# SOUPS · STEWS

Soup's on! For a light and
elegant first course, try our
Oriental Celery Soup. Or,
for a hearty meal, serve our
traditional Bouillabaise or
Seafood Gumbo.
Whether you choose these
or one of the other delicious
soups or stews, you'll
receive warm compliments
from all who sample them.

## Stock Up on Soup-Making Hints

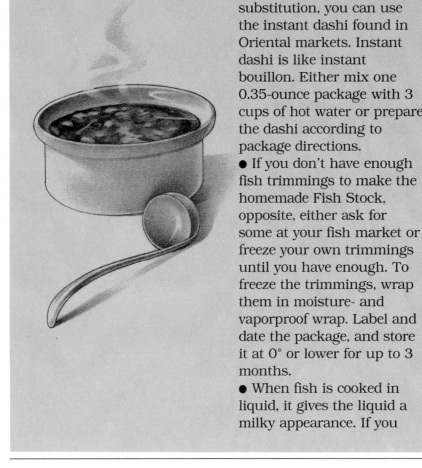

Here are some extra tips our home economists jotted down while testing the recipes in this chapter.

● Several of our recipes call for the homemade Fish Stock, opposite. For a quick substitution, you can use the instant dashi found in Oriental markets. Instant dashi is like instant bouillon. Either mix one 0.35-ounce package with 3 cups of hot water or prepare the dashi according to package directions.

● If you don't have enough fish trimmings to make the homemade Fish Stock, opposite, either ask for some at your fish market or freeze your own trimmings until you have enough. To freeze the trimmings, wrap them in moisture- and vaporproof wrap. Label and date the package, and store it at 0° or lower for up to 3 months.

● When fish is cooked in liquid, it gives the liquid a milky appearance. If you want your soup or stew to have a clear broth, poach the fish separately in a skillet or in another saucepan and add the fish to the soup or stew just before serving. If appearance isn't critical and you prefer to streamline the preparation, then cook the fish in the broth as directed.

● When cooking fish in soup, small 1-inch pieces will cook faster than whole fillets or steaks. As a general guide, when cooking pieces of fish in soup, allow about 2 minutes per ½-inch thickness of the fish pieces.

● To store leftover soup, simply place it in a covered container in the refrigerator for up to 2 or 3 days.

Reheat the soup over medium-low heat just till heated through. Be careful not to overheat it because the fish will overcook; cornstarch- or flour-thickened soups will also become thin in consistency.

# Fish Stock

3 pounds scaled drawn lean fish (see charts, pages 88–91), *or* fish bones, heads, *or* tails, *or* a combination
5 cups water
4 medium carrots, thinly sliced
4 stalks celery, chopped
2 medium onions, thinly sliced
⅔ cup dry white wine
¼ cup lemon juice
4 sprigs parsley
1½ teaspoons salt
4 whole black peppers
2 bay leaves

● If necessary, remove gills, break large bones, and cut fish to fit into a 5-quart Dutch oven. Add water, carrots, celery, onions, wine, lemon juice, parsley, salt, peppers, and bay leaves. Bring to boiling, then reduce heat. Simmer, uncovered, about 15 minutes or till surface is clear, skimming foam from surface. Then cover and simmer for 45 minutes more. Remove from heat.

● Line a colander with several layers of cheesecloth. Pour the mixture through colander. Discard solids. If desired, clarify stock (see below). Use stock as a base in soups or as the liquid for poaching fish.

● To store stock, cool slightly. Then cover and refrigerate for up to 2 days. Or freeze stock in covered plastic containers for up to 4 months. Makes 5½ cups.

**To clarify stock:** Stir together ¼ cup *cold water,* 1 *egg white,* and 1 crushed *eggshell.* Add to the strained stock and bring to boiling. Remove from heat; let stand for 5 minutes. Strain stock again through a colander lined with cheesecloth.

# Cioppino

*Created on the shores of Califorinia, this tomato stew teams fish and shellfish.*

8 fresh *or* frozen clams in shells
6 ounces fresh *or* frozen shelled shrimp
8 ounces skinless cod *or* sea bass fillets
1 small green pepper, cut into ½-inch pieces
¼ cup chopped onion
2 cloves garlic, minced
1 14½-ounce can sodium-free tomatoes, cut up
1 8-ounce can reduced-sodium tomato sauce
1 cup sliced fresh mushrooms
⅓ cup dry red wine
½ teaspoon dried basil, crushed
¼ teaspoon dried oregano, crushed

● Thaw clams and shrimp, if frozen. Wash clams well. Combine 8 cups *water* and 3 tablespoons *salt.* Add clams; soak 15 minutes. Drain and rinse. Discard water. Repeat soaking, draining, and rinsing twice. Devein shrimp. Cut fish into 1½-inch pieces. Cover and refrigerate shellfish and fish till needed.

● For stew, in a large saucepan combine green pepper, onion, garlic, and 2 tablespoons *water.* Cover and cook about 3 minutes or till onion is tender. Stir in *undrained* tomatoes, tomato sauce, mushrooms, wine, basil, oregano, ⅛ teaspoon *salt,* and ⅛ teaspoon *pepper.* Bring to boiling, then reduce heat. Cover and simmer for 20 minutes.

● Carefully add clams, shrimp, and fish. Return just to boiling, then reduce heat. Cover and simmer gently for 3 to 6 minutes or till fish is done and clams open. Discard any unopened clams. Makes 4 servings.

*Per serving:* 178 calories, 28 g protein, 243 mg sodium, 1 g fat, and 99 mg cholesterol.

Bouillabaisse

# Bouillabaisse

1 dozen fresh *or* frozen clams *or* mussels in shells, *or* a combination
2 8-ounce fresh *or* frozen lobster tails
12 ounces skinless monkfish *or* red snapper fillets
1 16-ounce can tomatoes
2½ cups Fish Stock (see recipe, page 57), *or* 1½ cups chicken broth *plus* one 8-ounce bottle clam juice
2 medium leeks, sliced
½ cup dry white wine
2 tablespoons snipped parsley
2 cloves garlic, minced
1 bay leaf
½ teaspoon dried thyme, crushed
¼ teaspoon fennel seed, crushed
¼ teaspoon thread saffron, crushed (optional)

● Thaw clams or mussels and lobster, if frozen. Wash clams or mussels well. If necessary, debeard mussels. Combine 8 cups *water* and 3 tablespoons *salt.* Add clams or mussels; let soak for 15 minutes, then drain and rinse. Discard the water. Repeat soaking, draining, and rinsing twice.

● Meanwhile, use kitchen shears to split the lobster tails lengthwise in half, cutting through the flesh and shells. Cut the fish into 1½-inch pieces. Cover and refrigerate the shellfish and fish till needed.

● For stew, cut up tomatoes. In a 5-quart Dutch oven combine *undrained* tomatoes, Fish Stock or chicken broth plus clam juice, leeks, wine, parsley, garlic, bay leaf, thyme, fennel, and saffron, if desired. Bring to boiling, then reduce heat. Cover and simmer for 10 minutes.

● Carefully add clams or mussels, lobster, and fish. Return just to boiling, then reduce heat. Cover and simmer gently for 3 to 6 minutes or till fish is done and clams or mussels open. Discard any unopened clams or mussels. Remove the bay leaf before serving. Makes 4 servings.

# Captain's Chowder

*Straight from the captain's kitchen comes this tomato-pasta chowder.*

1 12-ounce can (1½ cups) vegetable juice cocktail
½ cup medium shell macaroni
2 tablespoons grated Parmesan cheese
1 tablespoon dried minced onion
1 tablespoon instant chicken bouillon granules
½ teaspoon dried oregano, crushed
¼ teaspoon dried basil, crushed
Dash garlic powder
1 cup frozen mixed vegetables
12 ounces skinless cod, croaker, grouper, *or* red snapper fillets

● In a large saucepan combine 3 cups *water,* vegetable juice cocktail, macaroni, Parmesan cheese, onion, bouillon granules, oregano, basil, and garlic powder. Bring to boiling, then reduce heat. Cover and simmer for 15 minutes. Add frozen vegetables. Return to boiling, then reduce heat. Cover and simmer about 15 minutes more or till macaroni and vegetables are tender.

● Meanwhile, measure thickness of fish. Cut fish into 1-inch pieces. Carefully add the fish to the soup mixture. Return just to boiling, then reduce heat. Cover and simmer gently till fish is done (allow about 2 minutes per ½-inch thickness of fish).

● To serve, ladle soup into individual soup bowls. If desired, sprinkle with shredded cheddar cheese. Makes 4 servings.

# Seafood Chili Soup

*Tastes just like Texas chili, but without the beef.*

¼ cup chopped onion
¼ cup chopped green pepper
1 clove garlic, minced
1 tablespoon cooking oil
1 12-ounce can (1½ cups) tomato juice
1 cup water
1 8-ounce can red kidney beans
1 7½-ounce can tomatoes, cut up
1 6-ounce can sliced mushrooms, drained
1 tablespoon chili powder
½ teaspoon sugar
¼ teaspoon dried basil, crushed
⅛ to ¼ teaspoon crushed red pepper
1 bay leaf
1 pound skinless cod, cusk, *or* monkfish fillets

● In a medium saucepan cook onion, green pepper, and garlic in cooking oil till vegetables are tender.

● Stir in the tomato juice, water, *undrained* kidney beans, *undrained* tomatoes, mushrooms, chili powder, sugar, basil, red pepper, bay leaf, and ½ teaspoon *salt*. Bring to boiling; reduce heat. Cover and simmer for 15 minutes.

● Meanwhile, measure thickness of fish. Cut fish into 1-inch pieces. Carefully add fish to soup mixture. Return mixture just to boiling, then reduce heat. Cover and simmer gently till fish is done (allow about 2 minutes per ½-inch thickness of fish).

● To serve, remove bay leaf. Ladle soup into individual soup bowls. If desired, top with dairy sour cream. Makes 4 servings.

# Salmon and Tomato Bisque

12 ounces salmon, halibut, *or* swordfish steaks, cut 1 inch thick
1½ cups sliced fresh mushrooms
½ cup chopped onion
2 tablespoons butter *or* margarine
1 14½-ounce can tomatoes, finely cut up
¾ cup Fish Stock (see recipe, page 57) *or* chicken broth
¼ teaspoon salt
¼ teaspoon dried dillweed
Dash pepper
1½ cups light cream *or* milk
2 tablespoons cornstarch
2 tablespoons dry sherry
Fresh dill (optional)

● Remove skin and bones from fish. Cut fish into ¾-inch pieces.

● In a medium saucepan cook mushrooms and onion in butter or margarine till tender. Stir in tomatoes, Fish Stock or chicken broth, salt, dillweed, and pepper. Bring mixture just to boiling. Carefully add the fish. Return tomato mixture just to boiling, then reduce heat. Cover and simmer gently about 4 minutes or till fish is done.

● Meanwhile, in a small saucepan combine cream or milk and cornstarch. Cook and stir over medium heat till thickened and bubbly. Cook and stir for 2 minutes more. Gently stir cream mixture into tomato mixture. Then gently stir in the sherry. If necessary, cook mixture over medium-low heat till heated through. *Do not boil.*

● To serve, ladle soup into individual soup bowls. If desired, garnish with fresh dill. Makes 4 servings.

# Landlubber's Chowder

*Whether you're on land or at sea, this colorful, creamy chowder is sure to be a hit.*

12 ounces salmon *or* swordfish
    steaks, cut ¾ inch thick
1 medium tomato
3 slices bacon, halved
½ cup chopped onion
¼ cup chopped celery
1 cup water
1 cup loose-pack frozen
    mixed broccoli, carrots,
    and cauliflower
¾ cup cubed peeled potato
    (1 medium)
1 tablespoon instant chicken
    bouillon granules
1 teaspoon Worcester-
    shire sauce
⅛ teaspoon pepper
½ cup light cream
2 tablespoons all-purpose
    flour
1¼ cups milk

● Remove skin and bones from fish. Cut fish into ¾-inch pieces. Cover and refrigerate till needed. Cut tomato into 8 wedges, then seed and cut wedges crosswise in half. Set tomato aside.

● In a large saucepan cook the bacon till crisp. Drain, reserving *1 tablespoon* of drippings. Crumble bacon and set aside. Cook onion and celery in reserved drippings till nearly tender.

● Stir in water, frozen vegetables, potato, bouillon granules, Worcestershire sauce, and pepper. Bring to boiling, then reduce heat. Cover and simmer for 5 minutes.

● Combine cream and flour, then add it to potato mixture in pan. Stir in milk. Add fish. Bring almost to boiling, then reduce heat. Cover and simmer gently about 3 minutes or till fish is done. *Do not boil.* Stir in bacon and tomato. Makes 4 servings.

# Ragout de Sole

*The delicate orange flavor is a pleasant surprise.*

8 ounces skinless sole,
    flounder, *or* orange
    roughy fillets (about ½
    inch thick)
8 ounces fresh *or* frozen
    shelled shrimp
1 8-ounce package frozen cut
    asparagus
3 cups milk
2 tablespoons all-purpose
    flour
1 cup sliced fresh mushrooms
1 green onion, thinly sliced
½ teaspoon finely shredded
    orange peel
¼ teaspoon salt
⅛ teaspoon white pepper
2 tablespoons orange juice
1 cup cooked rice

● Cut fish into 1-inch pieces. Thaw shrimp, if frozen. Devein shrimp. Cover and refrigerate fish and shrimp till needed. Cook asparagus according to package directions, then drain and set asparagus aside.

● In a large saucepan combine about ¼ *cup* of the milk and flour till smooth, then stir in the remaining milk. Add fish, shrimp, mushrooms, onion, orange peel, salt, and pepper. Bring almost to boiling, then reduce heat. Cover and simmer gently for 2 to 3 minutes or till fish is done and shrimp turn pink. *Do not boil.* Stir in cooked asparagus, rice, and orange juice, and heat through. Makes 5 servings.

*Per serving:* 246 calories, 24 g protein, 281 mg sodium, 7 g fat, and 97 mg cholesterol.

# In-a-Hurry Curried Seafood Chowder

*No time to cook? Start with a can of soup, then add fish, apple, nuts, and sour cream for a hearty chowder in just minutes.*

12 ounces skinless cod, monk-fish, *or* tilefish fillets
1 cup milk
1 10¾-ounce can condensed New England clam chowder
1 medium apple, cored and chopped
1 teaspoon curry powder
1 teaspoon lemon juice
½ cup dairy sour cream
Chopped peanuts

● Measure thickness of fish. Cut fish into 1-inch pieces. Cover and refrigerate the fish till needed.

● In a medium saucepan stir milk into clam chowder. Stir in apple, curry powder, and lemon juice. Bring almost to boiling. Carefully add fish to soup mixture. Return almost to boiling, then reduce heat. Cover and simmer gently till the fish is done (allow about 2 minutes per ½-inch thickness of fish).

● Stir in sour cream and heat through. Ladle the soup into individual soup bowls and sprinkle with peanuts. Serves 3.

# Seafood Gumbo

*The full flavor of catfish is a good choice for this well-seasoned gumbo.*

12 ounces fresh *or* frozen cooked split crab legs
8 ounces fresh *or* frozen shelled shrimp
1 pound skinless catfish, cusk, haddock, *or* orange roughy fillets (½ to 1 inch thick)
½ cup margarine
½ cup all-purpose flour
2 cups chopped onion
1 cup chopped green pepper
5 cloves garlic, minced
4 cups chicken broth
1 28-ounce can tomatoes, cut up
2 cups sliced okra *or* one 10-ounce package frozen cut okra, thawed
1 teaspoon dried thyme, crushed
½ teaspoon ground red pepper
1 bay leaf
2 teaspoons filé powder
4 cups hot cooked rice

● Thaw crab and shrimp, if frozen. Remove crabmeat from shells, then cut crabmeat into bite-size pieces. Devein shrimp. Cut fish into 1-inch pieces. Cover and refrigerate the shellfish and fish till needed.

● For gumbo, in a 5-quart heavy Dutch oven melt margarine. Stir in flour. Cook and stir over medium-low heat for 20 to 25 minutes or till a dark reddish brown roux is formed. Add onion, green pepper, and garlic. Then continue cooking and stirring over medium-low heat about 15 minutes or till the vegetables are very tender.

● Gradually stir in chicken broth. Then stir in the *undrained* tomatoes, okra, thyme, pepper, and bay leaf. Bring to boiling, then reduce heat. Cover and simmer for 30 minutes.

● Carefully add crab, shrimp, and fish. Return just to boiling, then reduce heat. Cover and simmer gently for 2 to 4 minutes or till shrimp turns pink and fish is done. Remove from heat. Stir in filé powder.

● To serve, remove bay leaf. Spoon the gumbo over the hot rice in individual soup bowls. Makes 8 servings.

*Start with a roux (ROO) as the base for this traditional southern gumbo.*

### 1 Combining the margarine and flour

The roux, along with the okra and filé powder, thickens the Seafood Gumbo.

Make the roux from equal parts of margarine and flour. First melt the margarine, then stir in the flour till smooth. At the beginning of cooking, the roux will be a vanilla color.

### 2 Cooking the roux

Cook the roux slowly over medium-low heat for 20 to 25 minutes. Be sure to stir the roux *constantly* while it's cooking so that it doesn't scorch. If the roux burns, it won't thicken the gumbo.

To judge the doneness of the roux, compare its color to that of a tarnished copper penny. The roux will have the same rich brown color as the penny, as shown at right. It will also have a nutty aroma.

# Nacho-Snapper Chowder

*For a snappier cheese flavor, use sharp American cheese.*

1½ cups cubed peeled potatoes
  (2 medium)
½ cup chopped onion
½ cup chopped celery
1 pound skinless red snapper,
  cod, *or* monkfish fillets
1 16-ounce can cream-style
  corn
1 10-ounce can tomatoes and
  green chili peppers
2 cups milk
1½ cups shredded American
  cheese (6 ounces)
  Several dashes bottled hot
  pepper sauce (optional)
½ cup sliced pitted ripe
  olives
  Tortilla chips, slightly
  crushed

● In a large covered saucepan cook potatoes, onion, and celery in enough boiling water to cover till tender, then drain.

● Meanwhile, measure thickness of fish. Cut fish into 1-inch pieces. Add corn and *undrained* tomatoes and chili peppers to the potato-onion mixture. Bring just to boiling. Carefully add the fish. Return just to boiling, then reduce heat. Cover and simmer gently till the fish is done (allow about 2 minutes per ½-inch thickness of fish).

● Add milk, cheese, and hot pepper sauce, if desired. Stir gently till mixed. Cook over medium heat for 3 to 4 minutes or till cheese is melted and mixture is heated through. *Do not boil.* Stir in olives.

● To serve, ladle soup into individual soup bowls. Top with crushed tortilla chips. Makes 6 servings.

# Gruyère 'n' Cod Soup

*Gruyère (groo-YEHR) has a sweet nutty flavor like Swiss cheese.*

¼ cup finely chopped onion
¼ cup finely chopped carrot
2 tablespoons butter *or*
  margarine
¼ cup all-purpose flour
2 cups milk
1 teaspoon Dijon-style
  mustard
2 cups shredded Gruyère
  cheese *or* process Swiss
  cheese (8 ounces)
1 pound skinless cod, cusk,
  haddock, *or* pike fillets
1 14½-ounce can chicken
  broth
  Snipped chives *or* croutons
  (optional)

● In a large saucepan cook chopped onion and carrot in butter or margarine till vegetables are tender. Stir in flour. Then add milk and mustard. Cook and stir mixture over medium heat till thickened and bubbly. Add the cheese and continue cooking till cheese melts. Remove from heat and set aside.

● Meanwhile, measure thickness of fish. Cut fish into 1-inch pieces. In a medium saucepan bring the chicken broth just to boiling. Carefully add fish. Return just to boiling, then reduce heat. Cover and simmer gently till fish is done (allow about 2 minutes per ½-inch thickness of fish).

● Add the fish-broth mixture to the cheese mixture. Stir gently till well blended. If necessary, cook mixture over medium-low heat till heated through. *Do not boil.*

● To serve, ladle soup into individual soup bowls. If desired, top with snipped chives or croutons. Makes 4 servings.

# Cream of Potato Soup with Fish

*Combine the new with the old. Add fish and nutmeg to an old-time favorite soup.*

1½ cups cubed peeled potatoes (2 medium)
1 cup water
1 thinly sliced leek *or* ¼ cup chopped onion
1 teaspoon instant chicken bouillon granules
Dash white pepper
12 ounces skinless flounder *or* orange roughy fillets
1 13-ounce can (1⅔ cups) evaporated skim milk
⅛ teaspoon ground nutmeg

● In a medium saucepan combine the potatoes, water, leek or onion, bouillon granules, and pepper. Bring to boiling, then reduce heat. Cover and simmer for 10 minutes.

● Meanwhile, measure the thickness of the fish. Cut the fish into 1-inch pieces. Cover and refrigerate till needed.

● Transfer the cooked potato mixture to a blender container or food processor bowl. Cover and blend or process till smooth. Return to saucepan. Stir in milk and nutmeg. Add fish. Bring almost to boiling, then reduce heat. Cover and simmer gently till fish is done (allow about 2 minutes per ½-inch thickness of fish). *Do not boil.* Makes 4 servings.

*Per serving:* 195 calories, 22 g protein, 318 mg sodium, 1 g fat, and 45 mg cholesterol.

# German-Style Apple Stew

*Serve with rye bread and you've got a hearty fall or winter supper.*

1½ cups apple juice *or* apple cider
1½ cups water
2 medium carrots, halved lengthwise, then cut into 1½-inch pieces
1 stalk celery, sliced
½ cup sliced green onion
2 tablespoons cider vinegar
2 teaspoons instant chicken bouillon granules
1 teaspoon caraway seed
Dash pepper
1 pound skinless mahimahi *or* monkfish fillets (about 1 inch thick)
¼ of a small head cabbage, finely shredded (about 1¼ cups)
1 apple, cored and thinly sliced

● In a large saucepan combine apple juice or apple cider, water, carrots, celery, onion, vinegar, bouillon granules, caraway seed, and pepper. Bring mixture to boiling, then reduce heat. Cover and simmer for 10 minutes.

● Meanwhile, cut fish into 1-inch pieces. Carefully add fish to juice mixture. Return just to boiling, then reduce heat. Cover and simmer gently for 2 minutes. Add the cabbage and apple. Return just to boiling, then reduce heat. Cover and simmer gently about 2 minutes more or till fish is done and vegetables are nearly tender. Makes 4 servings.

# Cod-Vegetable Soup

*Chock-full of celery, carrot, cabbage, and zucchini.*

½ cup sliced celery
¼ cup chopped onion
2 tablespoons butter *or* margarine
3 cups Fish Stock (see recipe, page 57) *or* chicken broth
1 small zucchini, sliced ½ inch thick (1⅓ cups)
1 cup coarsely chopped cabbage
1 medium carrot, thinly sliced (½ cup)
¼ teaspoon dried basil, crushed
¼ teaspoon dried thyme, crushed
¼ teaspoon pepper
⅛ teaspoon dried rosemary, crushed
1 pound skinless cod, croaker, *or* drum fillets
Lemon wedges (optional)

● In a large saucepan cook the celery and onion in the butter or margarine till tender.

● Stir in Fish Stock or chicken broth, zucchini, cabbage, carrot, basil, thyme, pepper, and rosemary. Bring mixture to boiling, then reduce heat. Cover and simmer for 5 to 8 minutes or till vegetables are nearly tender.

● Meanwhile, measure thickness of fish. Cut fish into 1-inch pieces. Carefully add the fish to stock mixture. Return just to boiling, then reduce heat. Cover and simmer gently till fish is done (allow about 2 minutes per ½-inch thickness of fish).

● To serve, ladle soup into individual soup bowls. If desired, pass lemon wedges to squeeze over soup before eating. Serves 4.

# Fish 'n' Citrus Soup

*Sorrel (SAW-ruhl) adds a pleasant lemony flavor and a hint of green.*

3 cups Fish Stock (see recipe, page 57) *or* chicken broth
1 teaspoon finely shredded orange peel
⅓ cup orange juice
¼ cup chopped onion
1 tablespoon soy sauce
⅛ teaspoon white pepper
2 cloves garlic, minced
1 bay leaf
1½ pounds skinless cusk, haddock, *or* pike fillets, *or* halibut *or* shark steaks
1 cup finely chopped sorrel *or* spinach

● In a large saucepan combine Fish Stock or chicken broth, orange peel, orange juice, onion, soy sauce, pepper, garlic, and bay leaf. Bring mixture to boiling, then reduce heat. Cover and simmer for 5 minutes.

● Meanwhile, if using fish steaks, remove skin and bones. Measure thickness of fish. Cut fish into 1-inch pieces. Carefully add fish to soup mixture. Return just to boiling, then reduce heat. Cover and simmer gently till fish is done (allow about 2 minutes per ½-inch thickness of fish). Remove from heat. Remove bay leaf. Gently stir in sorrel or spinach till wilted. Makes 4 servings.

Cod-Vegetable Soup

# Chinese Hot and Sour Soup

*The hotness from the pepper and the tang from the rice wine vinegar get any menu off to a good start.*

4 cups chicken broth
½ cup canned whole straw
   mushrooms
½ cup canned bamboo shoots,
   halved lengthwise
1 small onion, sliced
¼ cup rice wine vinegar *or*
   white wine vinegar
1 tablespoon soy sauce
¼ teaspoon crushed red
   pepper
6 whole black peppers
12 ounces skinless pike, sea
   bass, *or* sea trout fillets
1 tablespoon cornstarch
1 tablespoon cold water
1 beaten egg
1 green onion, thinly sliced

● In a large saucepan combine the chicken broth, straw mushrooms, bamboo shoots, small sliced onion, vinegar, soy sauce, red pepper, and whole peppers. Bring to boiling, then reduce heat. Cover and simmer for 5 minutes.

● Meanwhile, measure thickness of the fish. For 1-inch-thick fillets, cut them into ½-inch pieces. For thinner fillets, cut them into 1-inch pieces. Carefully add fish to broth mixture. Return just to boiling, then reduce heat. Cover and simmer gently till fish is done (allow about 2 minutes per ½-inch thickness).

● Using a slotted spoon, remove fish from soup. Cover fish to keep it warm. Combine cornstarch and water, then add it to soup. Cook and stir soup over medium heat till thickened and bubbly. Cook and stir for 2 minutes more.

● Pour beaten egg in a thin stream into the hot soup. Stir gently till egg cooks and shreds finely. Remove saucepan from heat. Gently stir in fish.

● To serve, ladle soup into individual bowls. Top with sliced green onion. Makes 8 appetizer servings.

# Oriental Celery Soup

*Dashi (see tip, page 56) works equally as well as the Fish Stock in this first-course soup.*

3 cups Fish Stock, clarified
   (see recipe, page 57)
1 cup thinly bias-sliced celery
2 tablespoons dry sherry
2 thin slices gingerroot
1 green onion top
2 thin lime slices, halved

● In a medium saucepan combine Fish Stock, celery, sherry, and gingerroot. Bring to boiling, then reduce heat. Cover and simmer for 8 to 10 minutes or till celery is tender. Remove gingerroot from soup and discard.

● Meanwhile, cut green onion top lengthwise into fine julienne strips similar to thin noodles.

● To serve, stir green onion strips into soup. Then ladle soup into individual bowls. Add a lime slice half to each bowl. Makes 4 appetizer servings.

# SALADS

Looking for a creative light
meal? Just start with
cooked fish and add some
salad greens, a few
vegetables, and a little
dressing; you'll have
a fantastic meal in minutes.
Choose from a variety of
salads—everything
from Dilly Fish Slaw to
Tuna Taco Salads.

## Top with Croutons

Whether you're serving a salad or a soup, add one of these three croutons for an extra special touch.

● *Garlic Croutons:* In a large skillet melt ¼ cup *butter or margarine.* Add 1 large clove *garlic,* minced, and cook for 1 minute. Remove the skillet from the heat. Stir in 3¾ cups white, whole wheat, or pumpernickel *bread cubes* (about 5 slices of bread, cut into ½-inch cubes). Toss the cubes until they're coated with the butter mixture.

Spread the cubes in a large shallow baking pan into a single layer. Bake in a 300° oven for 10 minutes. Stir, then continue baking for 10 to 15 minutes more or till the bread cubes are dry and crisp. Cool before using on salads or soups.

You can keep these croutons for up to 1 month in a tightly covered container in the refrigerator. Makes 2 cups.

● *Dill Croutons:* Prepare the Garlic Croutons as directed, *except* omit the garlic. Cook 1 teaspoon dried *dillweed* in the melted butter or margarine.

● *Lemon Croutons:* Prepare the Garlic Croutons as directed, *except* omit the garlic. Cook 2 teaspoons finely shredded *lemon peel* in the melted butter or margarine.

## The Key to Crisp Salads

Lock freshness into your salads by cleaning the greens as soon as you bring them home.

Start by removing the core from iceberg lettuce or by separating the leaves of leafy greens. Then rinse the leaves under cold running water and pat them dry with a clean kitchen towel or paper towels.

Place the greens in a sealed plastic bag. Or put them in a covered plastic container designed for greens storage. You'll be able to store the greens in the refrigerator for as long as 3 to 4 days.

## What's in a Label?

When you're shopping, sometimes you'll find fish labeled "scrod." Actually, "scrod" is not a specific kind of fish. The term is sometimes used for cod or haddock that weighs under 2½ pounds.

# Halibut-Fruit Salad

*A fruit lover's dream: Oranges, pineapple, and apple tossed in
a rich curry dressing.*

1   10½-ounce can mandarin
    orange sections (water
    pack)
1   8-ounce can pineapple
    tidbits (juice pack)
12  ounces chilled cooked
    halibut, cusk, shark, sole,
    *or* tuna (see tip, page 10)
¼   cup reduced-calorie
    mayonnaise *or* salad
    dressing
¼   cup plain yogurt
½   teaspoon curry powder
1   medium apple, cored and
    chopped
    Lettuce leaves
¼   cup coconut, toasted

● Chill the cans of orange sections and pineapple tidbits in the
refrigerator till needed, then drain before using. Break or cut
fish into large chunks. (You should have about 2 cups.)

● For salad, in a large mixing bowl combine mayonnaise or
salad dressing, yogurt, and curry powder. Add orange sections,
pineapple, and apple. Toss lightly to coat. Add fish, then toss
lightly again.

● To serve, mound fruit mixture onto lettuce-lined salad plates.
Sprinkle with toasted coconut. Makes 4 servings.

*Per serving:* 275 calories, 25 g protein, 172 mg sodium, 10 g fat,
and 37 mg cholesterol.

# Spinach Salad with Pike

*Radicchio (rah-DEE-kee-oh), with its ruby red leaves and slightly bitter flavor, adds a
wonderful accent to this salad.*

1   8-ounce carton plain yogurt
⅓   cup mayonnaise *or* salad
    dressing
1   tablespoon brown mustard
1   teaspoon sugar
    Dash bottled hot pepper
    sauce
1¼  pounds chilled cooked pike,
    lake trout, *or* sea trout
    (see tip, page 10)
7   cups torn spinach *or*
    romaine
1   cup torn radicchio *or*
    shredded red cabbage
1   avocado, halved, seeded,
    peeled, and cut into
    crosswise slices
1   2¼-ounce can sliced pitted
    ripe olives, drained
1   green onion, sliced
3   hard-cooked eggs, cut into
    wedges

● For dressing, in a small mixing bowl stir together yogurt,
mayonnaise or salad dressing, mustard, sugar, hot pepper
sauce, and dash *salt*. If necessary, stir in 1 to 2 tablespoons *milk*
to make dressing of desired consistency. Cover and chill the
dressing while preparing the salad.

● For the salad, break the fish into large chunks. (You should
have about 3⅓ cups.) In a large mixing bowl combine fish,
spinach or romaine, radicchio or cabbage, avocado, and olives.
Toss lightly to mix.

● To serve, spoon spinach mixture onto salad plates. Drizzle
with dressing. Sprinkle with green onion and garnish with egg
wedges. Makes 6 servings.

## Tossed Cusk Salad with Lemon-Mustard Dressing

½ cup mayonnaise *or* salad dressing
1 teaspoon finely shredded lemon peel
1 tablespoon lemon juice
2 teaspoons Dijon-style mustard
Dash garlic powder
¼ cup whipping cream
1 pound chilled cooked cusk, cod, flounder, *or* orange roughy (see tip, page 10)
4 cups torn Bibb lettuce *or* Boston lettuce
1 cup torn sorrel *or* spinach
1 cup cherry tomatoes, halved
1 cup sliced fresh mushrooms
2 tablespoons capers, drained

● For the dressing, in a small mixing bowl stir together the mayonnaise or salad dressing, lemon peel, juice, mustard, and garlic. In another small bowl whip cream till soft peaks form. Then fold whipped cream into mayonnaise mixture. If necessary, stir in 1 to 2 tablespoons *milk* to make dressing of desired consistency. Cover and chill dressing while preparing salad.

● For the salad, break or cut the fish into large chunks. (You should have about 2⅔ cups.) In a large mixing bowl combine the fish, lettuce, sorrel or spinach, cherry tomatoes, and mushrooms. Toss lightly to mix.

● To serve, spoon lettuce mixture onto salad plates. Drizzle with dressing. Sprinkle with capers. Makes 4 servings.

## Fresh-Tuna Salade Niçoise

1½ cups cut fresh green beans
½ pound whole tiny new potatoes (4 to 6)
1 cup olive oil *or* salad oil
½ cup white wine vinegar
1 tablespoon dry mustard
1 tablespoon capers, drained and chopped (optional)
1 teaspoon dried basil, crushed
1 teaspoon dried oregano, crushed
2 cloves garlic, minced
12 ounces cooked tuna (see tip, page 10)
1 medium green pepper, cut into strips
1 cup cherry tomatoes, halved
¾ cup pitted ripe olives
2 cups torn romaine
2 cups torn Bibb lettuce *or* Boston lettuce
½ of a 2-ounce can anchovy fillets, drained and halved

● In a medium covered saucepan cook fresh beans in lightly salted boiling water for 10 minutes, then carefully add potatoes and return to boiling. Continue cooking about 15 minutes more or till vegetables are nearly tender, then drain. Rinse with cold water and drain again.

● Meanwhile, for the dressing, in a screw-top jar combine the oil, vinegar, dry mustard, capers (if desired), basil, oregano, and minced garlic. Cover and shake well.

● Break or cut tuna into large chunks. (You should have about 2 cups.) Place tuna in a dish just large enough to hold the fish in a single layer. Pour ½ *cup* of the dressing over the tuna.

● Quarter the potatoes. In a large bowl combine potatoes, beans, green pepper, tomatoes, olives, and ½ *cup* dressing. Toss lightly to coat. Cover and marinate tuna and vegetable mixtures separately in the refrigerator about 4 hours.

● To serve, combine romaine and Bibb or Boston lettuce. Spoon lettuce mixture onto large salad plates. Mound tuna mixture on top of lettuce. Then arrange vegetable mixture around tuna. Garnish with anchovies. Pass remaining dressing. Serves 4.

Fresh-Tuna Salade Nicoise

# Florida Haddock Salad

*Cool, crisp, and refreshing describe this tarragon-orange salad.*

12 ounces cooked haddock *or* tuna (see tip, page 10)
2 oranges
3 tablespoons salad oil
2 tablespoons tarragon vinegar
¼ teaspoon dried tarragon, crushed
⅛ teaspoon pepper
1 clove garlic, minced
2 cups torn iceberg lettuce
2 cups torn spinach
1 small red onion, sliced and separated into rings
½ cup sliced radishes

● Break or cut fish into large chunks. (You should have about 2 cups.) Place the fish in a dish just large enough to hold the fish in a single layer.

● Peel oranges. Over a small mixing bowl, section the oranges, reserving ¼ *cup* juice. Cover and refrigerate the orange sections till they are needed.

● For dressing, in a screw-top jar combine the reserved orange juice, oil, vinegar, tarragon, pepper, and garlic. Cover and shake well. Pour dressing over fish. Cover and marinate the fish in the refrigerator about 4 hours.

● For salad, in a large salad bowl combine lettuce, spinach, onion, radishes, and reserved orange sections. Add fish-dressing mixture to the salad. Toss lightly to coat. Makes 4 servings.

*Per serving:* 313 calories, 28 g protein, 89 mg sodium, 17 g fat, and 41 mg cholesterol.

# Romaine with Bass

*Jicama (HEE-kuh-muh), found in the produce section of the supermarket, has a delicate flavor like water chestnuts.*

12 ounces chilled cooked sea bass, cod, *or* shark (see tip, page 10)
7 cups torn romaine
5 ounces jicama, peeled and cut into 2-inch julienne sticks (about 1 cup), *or* one 8-ounce can sliced water chestnuts, drained
½ cup pine nuts *or* slivered almonds, toasted
⅓ cup light raisins
¼ cup salad oil
¼ cup dry sherry
2 tablespoons white wine vinegar
1 teaspoon sugar
¼ teaspoon garlic salt
¼ teaspoon dry mustard
Dash pepper

● Break or cut the fish into large chunks and set the fish aside. (You should have about 2 cups.) In a large salad bowl combine the romaine, jicama or water chestnuts, about *two-thirds* of the nuts, and raisins.

● For dressing, in a screw-top jar combine salad oil, sherry, vinegar, sugar, garlic salt, dry mustard, and pepper. Cover and shake well. Pour dressing over romaine mixture. Toss lightly to coat. Add the fish, then toss lightly again. Sprinkle with the remaining nuts. Makes 4 servings.

# Dilly Fish Slaw

*It's as simple as one, two, three! We added dill to bottled dressing for a quick fix-up.*

1 pound chilled cooked lean fish (see charts and tip, pages 88–91 and 10)
2 cups finely shredded cabbage
1 cup sliced fresh mushrooms
½ of a medium cucumber, thinly sliced (about ¾ cup)
1 medium tomato, cut into thin wedges
⅓ cup creamy cucumber reduced-calorie salad dressing
½ teaspoon dried dillweed

● Break or cut the fish into large chunks. (You should have about 2⅔ cups.)

● For salad, in a medium salad bowl combine the cabbage, mushrooms, cucumber, and tomato. Combine salad dressing and dill, then pour dressing mixture over cabbage mixture. Toss lightly to coat. Add fish, then toss lightly again. Serves 4.

*Per serving:* 184 calories, 26 g protein, 301 mg sodium, 5 g fat, and 59 mg cholesterol.

# Seafood-Stuffed Tomatoes

*Choose plump tomatoes as colorful containers for this bounty-of-the-sea salad.*

6 ounces chilled cooked lean fish (see charts and tip, pages 88–91 and 10)
½ cup chopped celery
¼ cup reduced-calorie mayonnaise *or* salad dressing
1 tablespoon snipped parsley
1 green onion, sliced
1 teaspoon Dijon-style mustard
1 teaspoon lemon juice
Dash bottled hot pepper sauce
6 ounces frozen split crab legs, thawed, shelled, and cut into chunks
Lettuce leaves
4 medium tomatoes

● Flake the fish. (You should have about 1 cup.) For the salad mixture, in a medium mixing bowl combine celery, mayonnaise or salad dressing, parsley, green onion, mustard, lemon juice, and hot pepper sauce. Stir till well blended. Add fish and crab, then toss lightly to mix.

● To serve, line salad plates with lettuce leaves. Cut ½ inch of the core from each tomato. Invert tomatoes. Cutting from the top to, *but not through,* the stem end, cut each tomato into 6 wedges. Place tomatoes on the plates. Spread wedges slightly apart, then fill with the salad mixture. Makes 4 servings.

*Per serving:* 127 calories, 13 g protein, 222 mg sodium, 6 g fat, and 39 mg cholesterol.

# Fish-Louis Salad in a Bread Bowl

⅓ cup mayonnaise *or* salad dressing

¼ cup thinly sliced green onion

2 tablespoons chili sauce

½ teaspoon lemon juice

¼ cup whipping cream

1 loaf unsliced round whole wheat *or* white bread (about 9 inches in diameter)

1 12-ounce package frozen split crab legs, thawed

8 ounces chilled cooked cod, halibut, *or* whiting (see tip, page 10)

2½ cups torn spinach *or* romaine

1 small tomato, cut into 8 wedges, then halved crosswise

● For the dressing, in a small mixing bowl stir together the mayonnaise or salad dressing, green onion, chili sauce, lemon juice, and dash *salt.* In another small bowl whip cream till soft peaks form. Then fold the whipped cream into mayonnaise mixture. Cover and chill dressing while preparing salad.

● For bread shell, insert toothpicks around top edge of loaf. Using the toothpicks as a guide, cut into, *but not through,* the loaf to form a cone. Remove the bread cone. Finish hollowing out the loaf, leaving a ¼-inch-thick shell. (Reserve the bread from the top and inside of the bread shell for another use, or make the croutons on page 70.)

● Remove crabmeat from shells, then cut crab into bite-size pieces. Break fish into large chunks. (You should have about 1⅓ cups of fish.) For the salad, in a large bowl combine spinach or romaine and tomato. Pour dressing over spinach mixture. Toss lightly to coat. Add crab and fish, then toss lightly again.

● To serve, spoon spinach mixture into bread shell. Then cut shell into quarters. Makes 4 servings.

**Making your bread bowl**

For your bowl, you'll need to start with a round, unsliced loaf of bread. To make the bread shell, insert toothpicks around the top of the loaf in about a 5-inch circle. Then, using the toothpicks as a guide, cut into the bread loaf at a 45-degree angle to form a cone. (Do not cut through the bottom of the loaf.) Remove the cone from the loaf. Then pull out the remaining bread from the inside of the loaf, leaving a ¼-inch-thick shell.

# Tuna Taco Salad

*For easy, no-mess tortilla bowls, use our baked method instead of frying them.*

½   cup plain yogurt *or* dairy
    sour cream
¼   cup mayonnaise *or* salad
    dressing
2   tablespoons sliced green
    onion
2   teaspoons chili powder
2   teaspoons lemon juice
1   pound chilled cooked tuna,
    cusk, pollack, salmon, sea
    bass, *or* sea trout (see
    tip, page 10)
10   cups torn iceberg lettuce
1   medium tomato, seeded and
    chopped
1   avocado, halved, seeded,
    peeled, and cut up
¼   cup sliced pitted ripe olives
    Tortilla Bowls (optional)
¼   cup shredded cheddar
    cheese (1 ounce)

● For dressing, stir together yogurt or sour cream, mayonnaise or salad dressing, onion, chili powder, lemon juice, and ¼ teaspoon *salt*. If necessary, stir in 2 to 3 tablespoons *milk* to make of desired consistency. Cover and chill while preparing salad.

● For salad, break or cut fish into large chunks. (You should have about 2⅔ cups.) In a large mixing bowl combine the lettuce, tomato, avocado, and olives. Pour dressing over mixture. Toss lightly to coat. Add fish, then toss lightly again.

● To serve, spoon lettuce mixture onto large salad plates or into Tortilla Bowls, if desired. Sprinkle with cheese. Serves 4.

**Tortilla Bowls:** Cut eight 10-inch circles from *heavy* foil. In a large skillet heat four 10-inch *flour tortillas,* one at a time, over low heat about 1 minute or just till pliable. Place each tortilla on 2 foil circles. Bring foil up, shaping foil and tortillas together into ruffled bowls. (The foil acts as a support.) Place bowls with foil onto an ungreased baking sheet. Bake in a 350° oven about 10 minutes or till crisp. Transfer bowls to a wire rack to cool. Remove foil before using.

# Curried Rice 'n' Fish Salad

*Also try stuffing this colorful salad into green pepper, artichoke, or tomato shells.*

12   ounces chilled cooked lean
    fish (see charts and tip,
    pages 88–91 and 10)
1   8-ounce carton plain yogurt
⅓   cup mayonnaise *or* salad
    dressing
2   tablespoons milk
2   teaspoons curry powder
⅛   teaspoon salt
1   cup cooked rice
1   small apple, cored and
    chopped
½   cup coarsely chopped
    peanuts
⅓   cup thinly sliced celery
⅓   cup raisins
    Lettuce leaves
1   medium tomato, cut into 8
    wedges

● Break or cut the fish into large chunks. (You should have about 2 cups.)

● For salad, in a large mixing bowl stir together the yogurt, mayonnaise or salad dressing, milk, curry powder, and salt. Add rice, apple, peanuts, celery, and raisins. Toss lightly to coat. Add fish, then toss lightly again. Cover and chill for 2 to 3 hours.

● To serve, mound rice mixture onto lettuce-lined salad plates. Garnish with tomato wedges. Makes 4 servings.

# Creamy Salmon-Potato Salad

*Chill the salad for several hours to let the many wonderful flavors blend together.*

5 medium potatoes (about
    1¾ pounds)
½ cup chopped *or* sliced celery
1 2¼-ounce can sliced pitted
    ripe olives, drained
4 green onions, thinly sliced
1¼ cups mayonnaise *or* salad
    dressing
1 tablespoon Dijon-style
    mustard
1 tablespoon vinegar
2 teaspoons celery seed
½ teaspoon salt
1 pound cooked salmon *or*
    tuna (see tip, page 10)
3 hard-cooked eggs, coarsely
    chopped
2 tablespoons diced pimiento
6 lettuce cups

● In a large covered saucepan cook potatoes in boiling water for 20 to 25 minutes or till just tender, then drain. Peel and cube the potatoes. Transfer to a large salad bowl. Add celery, olives, and green onions. Toss lightly to mix.

● For the dressing, in a small mixing bowl stir together the mayonnaise or salad dressing, mustard, vinegar, celery seed, and salt. Pour dressing over potato mixture. Toss lightly to coat.

● For salad, break or cut fish into large chunks. (You should have about 2⅔ cups.) Add fish, eggs, and pimiento to potato mixture. Toss lightly to mix. Cover and chill for 4 to 8 hours.

● To serve, if necessary, add a few tablespoons of *milk* to potato mixture and toss lightly to moisten. Serve potato mixture in lettuce cups. Makes 6 servings.

# Pasta 'n' Salmon Toss

*Serve croissants or corn muffins to complete this spinach-pasta-salad meal.*

¾ cup medium shell macaroni
    *or* corkscrew macaroni
¼ cup salad oil
3 tablespoons lemon juice
2 teaspoons Dijon-style
    mustard
¼ teaspoon salt
⅛ teaspoon garlic powder
⅛ teaspoon pepper
8 ounces chilled cooked
    salmon (see tip, page 10)
3 cups torn spinach
8 cherry tomatoes, halved
¾ cup sliced fresh mushrooms
1 tablespoon grated
    Parmesan cheese

● Cook pasta according to package directions, then drain. Place cooked pasta in a medium salad bowl.

● Meanwhile, for dressing, in a screw-top jar combine salad oil, lemon juice, mustard, salt, garlic powder, and pepper. Cover and shake well. Pour dressing over warm pasta. Toss lightly to coat. Cover and marinate pasta in the refrigerator for 2 to 3 hours, tossing mixture occasionally.

● For salad, break salmon into large chunks. (You should have about 1⅓ cups.) Add the spinach, tomatoes, and mushrooms to pasta-dressing mixture. Toss lightly to coat. Then add salmon and toss lightly again. Sprinkle with the grated Parmesan cheese. Makes 3 or 4 servings.

# APPETIZERS

It's party time. You supply
the friends and we'll supply
the good food ideas.
Whether you're having a
casual after-the-game
gathering or an elegant
open house, we've got
plenty of appetizers that are
sure to be welcome
additions. Together, we'll
make your party a success!

# A Quick Guide to Buying Salmon and Tuna

*If you're not sure which kind of fresh salmon or tuna is the best buy, here's the help you will need. Read below and we'll tell you how to match the color and flavor of a variety of salmon or tuna to the needs of your recipe.*

**Salmon** range from deep red to almost white in flesh color, and from mild to rich in flavor.

● *Chinook* or *king* is available fresh from March to October. The deep salmon- to white-colored raw flesh is beautiful in the Gravlax or Sushi (see recipes, page 86).

This variety also is an excellent choice for the Basil-Buttered Steaks on page 39. The oily-textured flesh broils and grills well because it needs little or no basting.

● *Chum* has a slightly coarser texture than the other salmons. You'll have the most luck finding fresh chum in August and September.

Depending on where it's caught and at what point it is in the spawning cycle, the color of this salmon can range from red to light pink. The delicate color is especially pretty in our Landlubber's Chowder, Salmon 'n' Cream Cheese Spread, or Calico Appetizer Quiche (see recipes, pages 61, 83, and 84).

● *Coho* is also referred to as *silver salmon* because of its silvery belly and sides. Yet its flesh is pink to orange-red in color.

Because of the small size of the farm-raised cohos (as small as 10 ounces), they're an excellent choice for individual servings of drawn or dressed salmon.

● *Norwegian salmon* is flown in fresh to the United States from Norway all year long. This mild-flavored salmon varies from pink to red in color and works well in most recipes.

● *Pink* is one of the least expensive salmons and is most often sold in cans.

● *Sockeye,* also known as *red salmon,* is primarily sold canned, but is also available fresh from June to November.

As with the chinook, the deep red color of sockeye makes it an excellent choice for the Gravlax and Sushi.

**Tunas** are so large they're usually cut into steaks. The different tunas can vary from strong to mild in flavor and from dark to light in color.

● *Albacore* is available fresh from June to October. Compared to the other tunas, albacore has the mildest flavor. It has white flesh. Because of its light color, it's very pretty in the Fresh-Tuna Salade Niçoise (see recipe and photograph, pages 72 and 73).

● *Bluefin,* along with the yellowfin, is red when raw and light tan when cooked.

Bluefin gets its name from the deep blue or green color on the top and sides of its body. It has a rich flavor and is commonly used in sushi.

You can buy this variety fresh from June to September.

● *Bonito,* weighing up to 5 pounds, is smaller than the other tunas. It's also less expensive and has a milder taste. The moderate fat content of this tuna makes it an excellent choice for baking, broiling, and grilling.

● *Yellowfin* is available fresh year-round in Hawaii and during the summer on the mainland. Because of its high fat content, yellowfin broils well.

# Halibut on Fresh Artichokes

*An elegant knife-and-fork appetizer.*

2 medium artichokes
   Lemon juice
⅔ cup dairy sour cream
2 tablespoons sliced green
   onion
2 tablespoons diced
   pimiento
1 tablespoon dry sherry
1 tablespoon milk
¼ teaspoon salt
¼ teaspoon celery seed
   Few dashes bottled hot
   pepper sauce
   Dash white pepper
6 ounces chilled cooked
   halibut *or* salmon (see tip,
   page 10)
1 hard-cooked egg, chopped
   Lettuce leaves
   Diced pimiento (optional)

● Wash and remove the coarse outer leaves from artichokes. Trim each stem even with base, then slice about 1 inch from each top. With kitchen shears, snip about ½ inch from the tips of remaining leaves. Brush lemon juice onto the cut edges.

● In a large saucepan bring about 2 inches of lightly salted water to boiling. Add artichokes. Cover and boil gently about 20 minutes or till the stem ends pierce easily with a fork. Drain the artichokes upside down on paper towels. Pull out center leaves. Scoop out fuzzy centers (chokes). Cover and chill artichokes.

● Meanwhile, in a mixing bowl stir together sour cream, onion, 2 tablespoons pimiento, sherry, milk, salt, celery seed, pepper sauce, and pepper. Break fish into chunks. (You should have about 1 cup.) If desired, reserve some chopped egg yolk for garnish. Add fish and remaining chopped egg to sour cream mixture. Toss lightly to coat. Cover and chill the fish mixture for up to 4 hours.

● To serve, cut each artichoke into fourths. Place artichoke pieces on small lettuce-lined plates. Spoon fish mixture onto artichokes. If desired, garnish with the reserved egg yolk or additional pimiento. Makes 8 appetizer servings.

# Fish-Stuffed Bacon Rolls

*Cut out last-minute preparation by chilling the unbaked rolls up to 3 hours before your party.*

8 ounces cooked flounder,
   mahimahi, *or* monkfish
   (see tip, page 10)
½ cup shredded peeled apple
1 tablespoon finely chopped
   onion
1 tablespoon snipped parsley
¼ teaspoon curry powder
⅛ teaspoon salt
⅛ teaspoon pepper
1 tablespoon milk
1 beaten egg yolk
¼ cup fine dry seasoned bread
   crumbs
12 slices bacon, halved
   crosswise

● Flake or finely chop the fish. (You should have about 1½ cups.) For stuffing, in a medium mixing bowl combine fish, apple, onion, parsley, curry powder, salt, and pepper. Add milk and egg yolk, then mix till well combined. Add bread crumbs, then mix well.

● For bacon rolls, *partially* cook the bacon. Drain bacon on paper towels. Place *1 rounded teaspoon* of stuffing onto an end of *each* piece of bacon. Roll bacon around stuffing. Secure with wooden toothpicks. If desired, cover and chill.

● To bake, place bacon rolls on a wire rack in a 15x10x1-inch baking pan. Bake in a 375° oven for 15 to 18 minutes or till the bacon is crisp. Serve immediately. Makes 24 bacon rolls or 8 to 12 appetizer servings.

Pompano 'n' Havarti Pastries

Salmon 'n' Cream Cheese Spread

# Salmon 'n' Cream Cheese Spread

8 ounces cooked salmon
  (see tip, page 10)
1 8-ounce container soft-style
  cream cheese with chives
  and onion
1 tablespoon lemon juice
2 teaspoons prepared
  horseradish
  Few dashes bottled hot
  pepper sauce
  Sesame or pumpernickel
  toast crackers

● Flake the salmon. (You should have about 1½ cups.) For the spread, in a blender container or food processor bowl place the cream cheese, lemon juice, horseradish, and hot pepper sauce. Cover and blend or process till smooth. Add salmon. Cover and blend or process just till well mixed. Transfer to a small serving bowl. Cover and chill for up to 8 hours.

● To serve, garnish with red caviar and celery leaf, if desired. Serve with toast crackers. Makes about 2 cups.

# Pompano 'n' Havarti Pastries

4 ounces cooked pompano,
  orange roughy, or sole
  (see tip, page 10)
¼ cup chopped onion
1 clove garlic, minced
1 tablespoon butter or
  margarine
1½ teaspoons all-purpose flour
¼ teaspoon dried dillweed
  Dash salt
¼ cup milk
½ cup shredded havarti cheese
  (2 ounces)
1 tablespoon finely chopped
  pimiento
1 11-ounce package piecrust
  mix (for 2-crust pie)
1 slightly beaten egg yolk
1 tablespoon water

● Flake the fish. (You should have about ¾ cup.) For filling, cook onion and garlic in butter or margarine till tender but not brown. Stir in flour, dillweed, and salt. Add milk. Cook and stir till thickened and bubbly. Cook and stir for 1 minute more. Add cheese; stir till melted. Remove from heat. Stir in the fish and pimiento; set filling aside. Prepare piecrust mix according to package directions. Divide dough in half. Assemble and bake pastries with or without using a madeleine pan. Serve warm. Makes 12 shell- or 24 triangle-shaped appetizers.

● *With madeleine pan:* On a lightly floured surface roll each dough half into a 16x8-inch rectangle. Place a dough rectangle over a madeleine pan with 2¼x1¼-inch shell molds. Gently press pastry into the shells. Fill each shell with about *1 tablespoon* of filling. Combine egg yolk and water; brush some of it around outlines of molds. Place other dough rectangle over the filled madeleine pan. Press with fingers around shells to seal. Using a fluted pastry wheel or knife, trim dough from edges of pan, then cut between the shells. Place pan in a 450° oven and bake for 15 minutes. Invert shells onto an ungreased baking sheet. Brush tops with egg mixture. Bake for 8 to 10 minutes more or till golden.

● *Without madeleine pan:* On a lightly floured surface roll each dough half into a 12x9-inch rectangle. Cut each rectangle into twelve 3-inch squares. Place about *1½ teaspoons* of filling on half of each square. Combine egg yolk and water; brush some of it around pastry edges. Fold squares in half, forming triangles. Press edges with the tines of a fork to seal. Brush with egg mixture. Bake in a 400° oven for 10 to 12 minutes or till golden.

# Calico Appetizer Quiche

5 ounces cooked cod, salmon, sea trout, *or* sole (see tip, page 10)
3 eggs
1¼ cups light cream
¾ teaspoon dry mustard
½ teaspoon salt
½ teaspoon finely shredded lemon peel
2 tablespoons diced pimiento
½ cup shredded Swiss cheese (2 ounces)
½ cup shredded Colby cheese (2 ounces)
1 tablespoon all-purpose flour
1 stick piecrust mix (for 1-crust pie)
⅓ cup sliced green onion

● Flake the fish. (You should have about 1 cup.) For the egg mixture, in a medium mixing bowl beat eggs. Stir in cream, dry mustard, salt, and lemon peel. Then stir in fish and pimiento. In another bowl combine Swiss and Colby cheeses. Add the flour and toss lightly to coat. Add cheese mixture to egg mixture and stir till combined. Set egg mixture aside.

● Prepare piecrust mix according to the package directions. On a lightly floured surface roll pastry dough into a 12-inch circle. Place pastry in a 10-inch fluted quiche dish or pie plate, then flute edges. *Do not prick pastry.* Line pastry shell with a double thickness of *heavy* foil. Bake in a 450° oven for 8 minutes. Remove foil and bake for 3 to 5 minutes more or till pastry is *nearly* done. Remove pastry from oven.

● Reduce oven temperature to 325°. Pour egg mixture into *hot* pastry shell. Sprinkle with onion. Bake in the 325° oven for 35 to 40 minutes or till a knife inserted near center comes out clean. (If necessary, cover edges of crust with foil to prevent overbrowning.) Let stand about 10 minutes before serving. Cut into small wedges to serve. Makes 12 appetizer servings.

# Nutty Fish Nuggets

1 pound skinless cod, flounder, orange roughy, *or* sole fillets (¼ to ½ inch thick)
Shortening *or* cooking oil for deep-fat frying
¾ cup broken walnuts
¼ cup all-purpose flour
3 tablespoons grated Parmesan cheese
¼ teaspoon salt
1 beaten egg
1 tablespoon milk
⅓ cup all-purpose flour
Peppy Cocktail Sauce, Creamy Tarragon Sauce, *or* Green Chili Salsa (see recipes, right and pages 52 and 53)

● Cut fish into about 1½x1-inch pieces. Cover and refrigerate till needed. In a medium saucepan or a deep-fat fryer heat 3 inches of shortening or cooking oil to 375°.

● Meanwhile, for nut coating, in a blender container or food processor bowl place walnuts, ¼ cup flour, Parmesan cheese, and salt. Cover and blend or process till a fine powder forms. Then transfer nut coating to a shallow dish.

● In another shallow dish combine egg and milk. Dip fish into the ⅓ cup flour, then dip into egg mixture. Roll fish in nut coating. Fry fish in the hot fat (375°), ¼ at a time, for 2 to 3 minutes or till fish is done and coating is light brown. Drain fish on paper towels. Serve fish nuggets with desired sauce. Makes about 24 fish nuggets or 6 to 8 appetizer servings.

**Peppy Cocktail Sauce:** In a mixing bowl combine ⅓ cup *chili sauce,* ⅓ cup *catsup,* 1 tablespoon *lemon juice,* 2 teaspoons prepared *horseradish,* 2 teaspoons *Worcestershire sauce,* ½ teaspoon *dry mustard,* and ⅛ teaspoon *pepper.* Stir till well blended. Cover and chill till serving time. Makes ¾ cup.

# Seviche

*The marinade "cooks" the fish.*

½ pound skinless haddock, pike, *or* red snapper fillets, *or* halibut steaks (¼ to ½ inch thick)
1 medium onion, chopped
1 cup lime *or* lemon juice
¼ cup cooking oil
2 tablespoons capers, drained
2 teaspoons sugar
1 to 2 teaspoons crushed red pepper
¼ teaspoon salt
1 medium tomato, cut into 8 wedges, seeded, then halved crosswise
1 tablespoon snipped cilantro *or* parsley
2 large avocados, halved, seeded, peeled, and sliced crosswise

● If using fish steaks, remove skin. Cut fish into ½-inch pieces. Place *raw* fish and onion in a plastic bag. Place bag in a bowl.

● For marinade, combine juice, oil, capers, sugar, red pepper, and salt. Pour over fish and onion. Close bag; marinate in the refrigerator for *at least* 24 hours or till all fish pieces are opaque, turning bag occasionally.

● About 1½ hours before serving, add tomato and cilantro or parsley to fish mixture in bag. Close bag and turn bag gently to coat mixture with marinade. Refrigerate till serving time.

● To serve, arrange the avocado slices around the outer edges of small plates. (Place the rounded edges of the avocado slices toward the outer edges of the plates, forming petallike shapes.) Using a slotted spoon, spoon the fish mixture into centers. Makes 6 appetizer servings.

# Pickled Fish

*If your fillets are thicker than ½ inch, then just slice them to the thickness you need.*

1 to 1½ pounds skinless cod, flounder, pike, *or* sole fillets (¼ to ½ inch thick)
3 cups water
1 cup white vinegar
¼ cup pickling salt
1½ cups white vinegar
¾ cup water
½ cup sugar
1 tablespoon mixed pickling spice
Assorted crackers

● Cut fish into about 1½x¾-inch pieces. In a large mixing bowl combine the 3 cups water, 1 cup white vinegar, and pickling salt. Stir mixture till the salt dissolves. Stir in fish. Cover and refrigerate for *at least* 48 hours or till all fish pieces are opaque.

● Drain fish, discarding the salt liquid. Place fish in a colander and run *cold* water over it to rinse. Place fish in two 1-pint jars.

● In a saucepan combine 1½ cups white vinegar, ¾ cup water, sugar, and pickling spice. Bring to boiling, stirring occasionally. Remove from heat and cool slightly. Pour mixture over fish in jars to cover. Wipe jar rims and cover tightly. Refrigerate for 5 days before serving. Fish can be stored for up to 3 weeks total.

● To serve, drain fish and serve with assorted crackers. Makes 2½ to 3¼ cups or 12 to 16 appetizer servings.

# Gravlax

1 bunch fresh dill (1½ ounces)
¼ cup salt
¼ cup sugar
1 tablespoon whole white peppers (peppercorns), crushed
2 1-pound salmon fillets with skin (½ to ¾ inch thick)
  Dark bread
  Cream cheese
  Capers, drained

● Coarsely chop the dill and set aside. In a small mixing bowl combine the salt, sugar, and crushed peppers.

● Lay 1 fillet, skin side down, in a baking dish. Top fillet with dill, then sprinkle with salt mixture. Form a sandwich by placing the thin end of the second fillet, skin side up, on top of the thick end of the other fillet so that the sandwich is of even thickness. Cover with foil and refrigerate for *at least* 4 days or till the salmon is translucent and firm, basting with the juices occasionally. Salmon can be stored in the refrigerator for up to 1 week total.

● To serve, remove salmon from juices. Remove dill mixture from fillets. Pat dry with paper towels. Place fillets, skin side down, on a cutting board. Holding a knife at a 45-degree angle, cut fillets across the grain into paper-thin slices without cutting through skin. Then cut slices from the skin. Serve with bread, cream cheese, and capers. Makes 16 to 20 appetizer servings.

# Sushi

3½ cups water
1½ cups short grain rice
¾ teaspoon salt
¼ cup rice *or* white vinegar
3 tablespoons sugar
3 tablespoons sweet rice wine (mirin) *or* dry sherry
8 ounces *extremely fresh* skinless saltwater fillets (see charts, pages 88–91)*
8 sheets amanori seaweed (about 8 inches square)
½ of a small cucumber, sliced paper-thin
1 medium avocado, halved, seeded, peeled, and cut into julienne sticks; 2 ounces cooked asparagus tips; *or* 2 ounces pickled daikon, cut into julienne sticks; *or* a combination of the three
2 tablespoons red *or* black caviar (optional)

● In a medium saucepan combine water, *uncooked* rice, and salt. Bring to boiling; reduce heat. Cover and simmer for 15 minutes. Remove from heat. Stir in vinegar, sugar, and rice wine or sherry. Cover and cool to room temperature. Meanwhile, holding a knife at a 30-degree angle, cut fillets across the grain into ¼-inch-thick slices. Refrigerate fish till needed.

● To toast seaweed, place sheets in a single layer on the rack of an unheated broiler pan. Broil 5 to 6 inches from the heat for 8 to 10 seconds or till color changes to green. Lay toasted seaweed on a flat surface. Spread about ½ *cup* of the rice mixture over entire surface of each sheet, reserving a 1½-inch margin at one edge of each sheet. About 1½ inches from opposite edge, overlap cucumber slices. Top with 2 or 3 slices of fish; avocado, asparagus, or daikon; and caviar, if desired. Roll up jelly-roll style, starting from the edge near the cucumbers and pressing the seaweed together to seal. Cut each roll into 6 pieces. Either serve immediately or cover and chill for up to 2 hours. Makes 48 pieces or 16 to 24 appetizer servings.

*Use only fresh saltwater or cooked fish (see charts and tip, pages 88–91 and 10). *Do not substitute* raw freshwater or frozen fish.

*In Japanese, sushi means "vinegared rice."*

**1 Making the sushi roll**
To assemble the Sushi, overlap the cucumber slices on top of the rice mixture. Then top with fish; avocado, asparagus, or daikon; and caviar. Roll up the seaweed, jelly-roll style, starting at the edge near the cucumbers. To seal, press the edge without the rice around the roll.

**2 Presenting an attractive platter**
For a colorful assortment of Sushi, mix and match the vegetables, avocado, caviar, and different kinds of fish. In the Sushi shown, we used pink-flesh varieties of salmon and sea bass. Other good choices are tuna, halibut, and red snapper.

For an authentic touch, spread a bit of wasabi paste underneath the cucumber. Wasabi paste is a bright green Japanese horseradish available in Oriental markets. It's very hot, so use it sparingly.

# FRESHWATER FISH

| Species | Market Forms | Common Size |
|---|---|---|
| **Carp** | Dressed, Fillets | 2–8 lbs. |
| **Catfish** | Dressed, Steaks, Fillets | 8 oz.–6 lbs. |
| **Lake Perch** | Drawn, Dressed, Fillets | 4–12 oz. |
| **Lake Trout** | Drawn, Steaks, Fillets | 2–8 lbs. |
| **Pike** | Drawn, Dressed, Fillets | 1–10 lbs. |
| **Smelt** | Drawn, Dressed, Frozen Dressed | 4–15 per lb. |
| **Rainbow Trout** | Drawn, Drawn and Partially Boned, Dressed, Fillets | 5–12 oz. |
| **Whitefish** | Drawn, Dressed, Steaks, Fillets | 1½–4 lbs. |

# SALTWATER FISH

| Species | Market Forms | Common Size |
|---|---|---|
| **Atlantic Ocean Perch** | Drawn, Fillets, Frozen Unbreaded Portions | 8 oz.–2 lbs. |
| **Bluefish** | Drawn, Dressed, Fillets | 3–6 lbs. |
| **Butterfish** | Dressed, Fillets | 4 oz.–1 lb. |
| **Cod** | Drawn, Dressed, Steaks, Fillets, Frozen Unbreaded Portions | 1½–20 lbs. |
| **Croaker** | Drawn, Dressed, Fillets | 4 oz.–2 lbs. |
| **Cusk** (Ocean Catfish) | Dressed, Steaks, Fillets | 1½–5 lbs. |
| **Drum** | Drawn, Dressed, Fillets | 2–10 lbs. |
| **Flounder** | Drawn, Dressed, Fillets, Frozen Unbreaded Portions | 8 oz.–10 lbs. |
| **Greenland Turbot** | Fillets | 8–15 lbs. |
| **Grouper** | Drawn, Dressed, Steaks, Fillets | 3–20 lbs. |
| **Haddock** | Drawn, Dressed, Fillets, Frozen Unbreaded Portions | 2½–5 lbs. |
| **Halibut** | Drawn, Dressed, Steaks | 5–80 lbs. |

| Fat Content* | Texture | Flavor | Substitute Suggestions |
|---|---|---|---|
| Low to Moderate | Firm | Mild | Cod, Drum, Haddock, Redfish |
| Low | Firm | Mild | Cusk |
| Low | Firm | Mild | Atlantic Ocean Perch, Pike, Rainbow Trout |
| Moderate to High | Firm | Mild | Pike, Sea Trout, Whitefish |
| Low | Firm | Mild | Cod, Orange Roughy, Whitefish |
| High | Firm | Mild | No Substitute |
| Moderate to High | Firm | Delicate | Coho Salmon, Pike, Sea Trout |
| High | Firm | Delicate | Haddock, Lake Trout, Pike |

| Fat Content* | Texture | Flavor | Substitute Suggestions |
|---|---|---|---|
| Low | Firm | Delicate | Lake Perch, Rainbow Trout, Sea Bass |
| High | Fine | Mild | Flounder, Lake Trout, Pike |
| High | Fine | Mild | Pompano, Porgy |
| Low | Firm | Delicate | Haddock, Halibut, Pike, Pollack |
| Low | Firm | Mild | Cod, Cusk, Drum |
| Low | Firm | Delicate | Catfish, Cod, Croaker |
| Low | Firm | Mild | Carp, Croaker, Cusk, Redfish |
| Low | Fine | Delicate | Pike, Sole, Whitefish, Whiting |
| Low | Fine | Mild | No Substitute |
| Low | Firm | Mild | Cod, Monkfish, Sea Bass |
| Low | Firm | Delicate | Cod, Lake Trout, Sea Trout, Whitefish |
| Low | Firm | Delicate | Flounder, Sea Bass, Sole |

*Low is less than 5% fat; moderate is 5% to 10% fat; and high is greater than 10% fat.

# SALTWATER FISH (continued)

| Species | Market Forms | Common Size |
|---|---|---|
| **Lingcod** | Dressed, Steaks, Fillets | 5–20 lbs. |
| **Mackerel** | Drawn, Steaks, Fillets | 8 oz.–25 lbs. |
| **Mahimahi** (Dolphinfish) | Steaks, Fillets | 2–40 lbs. |
| **Monkfish** | Fillets, Tails | Up to 50 lbs. |
| **Mullet** | Drawn, Fillets | 1–3 lbs. |
| **Orange Roughy** | Fillets | 2–5 lbs. |
| **Pollack** | Drawn, Dressed, Steaks, Fillets, Frozen Unbreaded Portions | 4–12 lbs. |
| **Pompano** | Drawn, Fillets | 1½–4 lbs. |
| **Porgy** | Drawn, Dressed, Fillets | 1–2 lbs. |
| **Redfish** | Dressed, Fillets | Up to 10 lbs. |
| **Red Snapper** | Dressed, Fillets | 2–8 lbs. |
| **Rockfish** (Pacific Snapper) | Drawn, Dressed, Fillets | 1–5 lbs. |
| **Salmon** (also see tip, page 80) | Dressed, Steaks, Fillets | 10 oz.–30 lbs. |
| **Sea Bass** | Drawn, Dressed, Fillets, Steaks | 1½–40 lbs. |
| **Sea Trout** | Drawn, Fillets | 1–6 lbs. |
| **Shad** | Drawn, Fillets | 3–4 lbs. |
| **Shark** | Steaks, Fillets | 15–200 lbs. |
| **Sole** | Dressed, Fillets, Frozen Unbreaded Portions | 8 oz.–6 lbs. |
| **Swordfish** | Steaks | 100–200 lbs. |
| **Tilefish** | Drawn, Dressed, Fillets | 4–7 lbs. |
| **Tuna** (also see tip, page 80) | Drawn, Steaks, Fillets | 8 oz.–150 lbs. |
| **Whiting** | Drawn, Dressed, Steaks, Fillets, Frozen Unbreaded Portions | 12 oz.–8 lbs. |

| Fat Content* | Texture | Flavor | Substitute Suggestions |
|---|---|---|---|
| Low | Firm | Delicate | Cod, Grouper, Pike |
| High | Firm | Rich | Swordfish, Tuna |
| Moderate | Firm | Mild | Bluefish |
| Low | Firm | Mild | Cusk |
| Moderate to High | Firm | Mild | No Substitute |
| Low | Firm | Delicate | Cod, Sea Bass, Sole |
| Low to Moderate | Firm | Mild | Cod, Flounder, Pike |
| Moderate | Firm | Mild | Atlantic Ocean Perch, Butterfish, Sole |
| Low | Firm | Delicate | Atlantic Ocean Perch, Butterfish, Lake Perch |
| Low | Firm | Mild | Carp, Croaker, Drum |
| Low | Firm | Mild | Lake Trout, Rockfish, Whitefish |
| Low | Firm, Chewy | Mild | Atlantic Ocean Perch, Cod, Drum, Red Snapper, Tilefish |
| Moderate to High | Firm | Mild to Rich | Swordfish, Tuna |
| Moderate | Firm | Delicate | Cod, Orange Roughy, Sea Trout |
| Moderate | Firm | Delicate | Cod, Haddock, Pike, Pollack |
| High | Firm | Mild | Butterfish, Flounder, Whiting |
| Low | Firm, Dense | Mild | Salmon, Sea Bass, Swordfish, Tuna |
| Low | Fine | Delicate | Flounder, Pike |
| Low to Moderate | Firm, Dense | Mild | Sea Bass, Shark, Tuna |
| Low | Firm | Mild | Rockfish |
| Moderate to High | Firm | Mild to Rich | Mackerel, Salmon, Swordfish |
| Low | Firm | Mild | Flounder, Pike, Pollack, Sole |

*Low is less than 5% fat; moderate is 5% to 10% fat; and high is greater than 10% fat.

# Index

# Index

# Index

If you want to add even more great-tasting fish recipes to your collection, turn to BETTER HOMES AND GARDENS® *All-Time Favorite Fish and Seafood Recipes.* In it you'll find many recipes that cater to your special tastes— everything from old standbys, such as Tuna-Noodle Casserole, to more elegant entertaining favorites, such as Lobster Quiche.